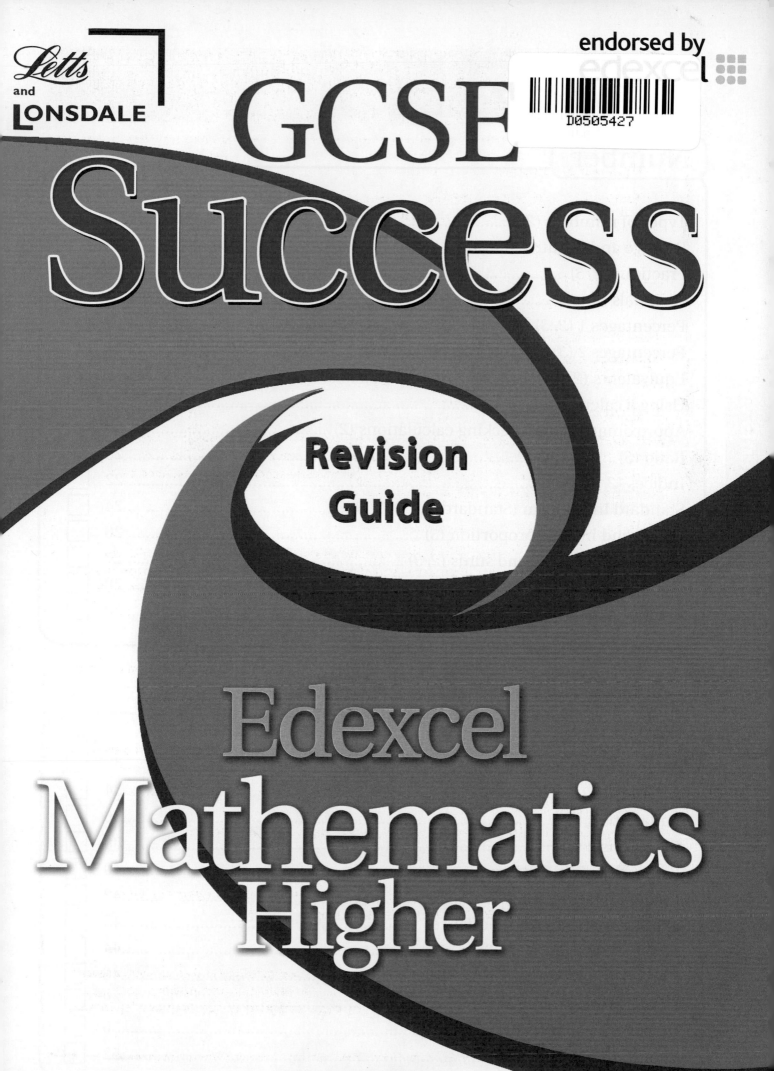

Letts
and
LONSDALE

GCSE
Success

endorsed by
edexcel

D0505427

Revision
Guide

Edexcel
Mathematics
Higher

Fiona C. Mapp

Contents

Number

Algebra

Shape, space and measures

	Revised

Handling data

	Revised

If you are following the modular specification (2381), the numbers in brackets indicate which unit(s) the content of each page is relevant to.

MATHS SUCCESS

Contents

Types of numbers

Square roots and cube roots

$\sqrt{}$ is the square root sign. Taking the square root is the opposite of squaring.

For example, $\sqrt{25} = \pm 5$ since $5^2 = 25$, or $(-5)^2 = 25$.

$\sqrt[3]{}$ is the cube root sign. Taking the cube root is the opposite of cubing.

For example, $\sqrt[3]{8} = 2$ since $2^3 = 8$.

Squares and cubes

Square numbers

Any number raised to the **power 2** gives a **square number**. For example, $6^2 = 6 \times 6 = 36$ (six squared).
Square numbers include:

1	4	9	16	25	36	49	64
(1×1)	(2×2)	(3×3)	(4×4)	(5×5)	(6×6)	(7×7)	(8×8)

81	100	121	144	169	196	225
(9×9)	(10×10)	(11×11)	(12×12)	(13×13)	(14×14)	(15×15)

Square numbers can be illustrated by drawing squares.

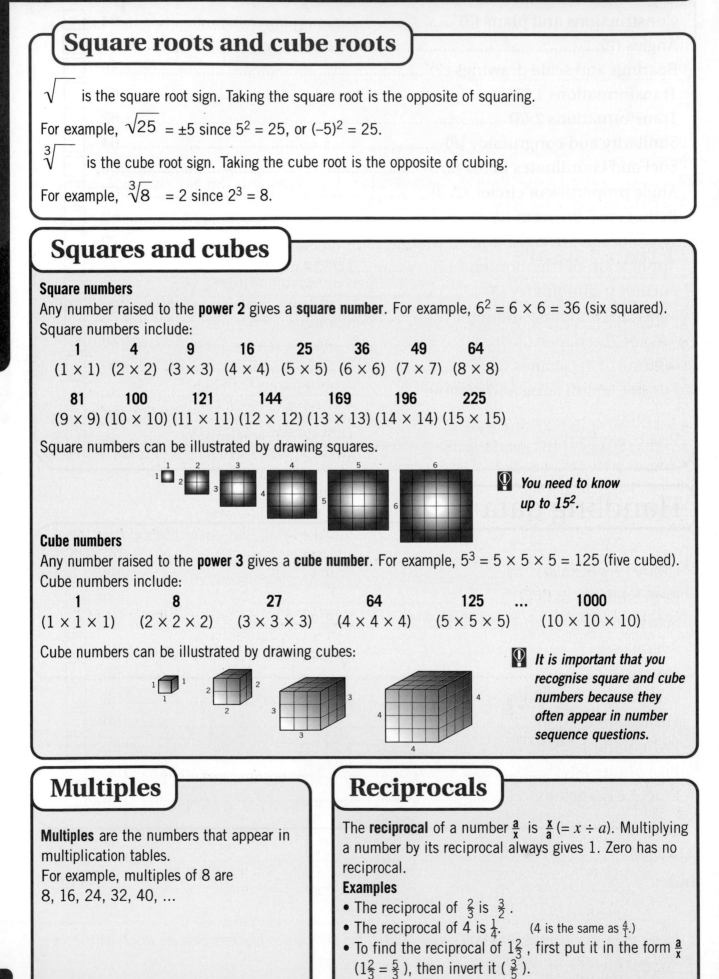

💡 *You need to know up to 15^2.*

Cube numbers

Any number raised to the **power 3** gives a **cube number**. For example, $5^3 = 5 \times 5 \times 5 = 125$ (five cubed).
Cube numbers include:

1	8	27	64	125	...	1000
$(1 \times 1 \times 1)$	$(2 \times 2 \times 2)$	$(3 \times 3 \times 3)$	$(4 \times 4 \times 4)$	$(5 \times 5 \times 5)$		$(10 \times 10 \times 10)$

Cube numbers can be illustrated by drawing cubes:

💡 *It is important that you recognise square and cube numbers because they often appear in number sequence questions.*

Multiples

Multiples are the numbers that appear in multiplication tables.
For example, multiples of 8 are
8, 16, 24, 32, 40, ...

Reciprocals

The **reciprocal** of a number $\frac{a}{x}$ is $\frac{x}{a} (= x \div a)$. Multiplying a number by its reciprocal always gives 1. Zero has no reciprocal.

Examples
- The reciprocal of $\frac{2}{3}$ is $\frac{3}{2}$.
- The reciprocal of 4 is $\frac{1}{4}$.   (4 is the same as $\frac{4}{1}$.)
- To find the reciprocal of $1\frac{2}{3}$, first put it in the form $\frac{a}{x}$
  ($1\frac{2}{3} = \frac{5}{3}$), then invert it ($\frac{3}{5}$).

Factors and primes

Factors

Factors are whole numbers which divide exactly into another number. For example, the factors of 20 are 1, 2, 4, 5, 10, 20. To find all the factors of a number, start at 1 and divide by each whole number in turn. Factors can be matched up into factor pairs. For example, for the factors of 20:

```
1 2  3  4  5  6  7  8  9 10 11 12 13 14 15 16 17 18 19 20
```

So $1 \times 20 = 20$ $2 \times 10 = 20$ $4 \times 5 = 20$

Prime numbers

A **prime number** is a number which has only two factors, 1 and itself. Note that 1 is not a prime number. The prime numbers up to 20 are 2, 3, 5, 7, 11, 13, 17 and 19.

Prime factors

These are factors that are prime.
All whole numbers can be written as products of their prime factors.

Example

The diagram below shows the prime factors of 360.
• Divide 360 by its first prime factor, 2.
• Divide 180 by its first prime factor, 2.
• Keep on going until the final number is prime.
As a product of its prime factors,
360 can be written as:
$2 \times 2 \times 2 \times 3 \times 3 \times 5 = 360$
or $2^3 \times 3^2 \times 5 = 360$
in **index** notation (using powers).

Highest common factor (HCF)

The **largest factor** that two numbers have in common is called the **HCF**.

Example

Find the HCF of 84 and 360.
• Write the numbers as products of their prime factors.
$84 =\ \ (2) \times (2) \times\ \ (3)\ \ \times 7$
$360 = (2) \times (2) \times 2 \times (3) \times 3 \times 5$
• Ring the common factors
• These give the HCF $= 2 \times 2 \times 3 = 12$

Least common multiple (LCM)

The **LCM** is the lowest number that is a multiple of two or more numbers.

Example

Find the LCM of 6 and 8.
• Write the numbers as products of their prime factors.
$8 = 2 \times 2 \times (2)$
$6 =\ \ \ \ \ \ \ \ (2) \times 3$
• 8 and 6 have a common prime factor of 2. It is only counted once.
• The LCM of 6 and 8 is $2 \times 2 \times 2 \times 3 = 24$

QUICK TEST

❶ List the prime numbers up to 20.

❷ Find the HCF and LCM of 24 and 60.

❸ Find a) $\sqrt{64}$ b) $\sqrt[3]{216}$

❹ Write down the reciprocals of
a) $\frac{9}{12}$ b) $\frac{x}{p}$

Positive and negative numbers

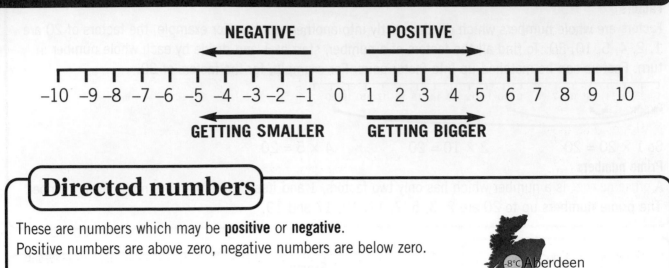

NEGATIVE ← POSITIVE →

–10 –9 –8 –7 –6 –5 –4 –3 –2 –1 0 1 2 3 4 5 6 7 8 9 10

GETTING SMALLER   GETTING BIGGER

Directed numbers

These are numbers which may be **positive** or **negative**.
Positive numbers are above zero, negative numbers are below zero.

Examples

–10 is smaller than –8. $-10 < -8$
–4 is bigger than –8. $-4 > -8$
2 is bigger than –6. $2 > -6$

Directed numbers are often seen on the weather
forecast in winter. Quite often the **temperature** is below 0.
Aberdeen is the coldest on this forecast map at –8°C.
London is 6°C warmer than Manchester.

-8°C Aberdeen

-4°C Manchester

2°C London

Integers

The **integers** are the set of numbers $\{\ldots -3, -2, -1, 0, 1, 2, 3, \ldots\}$.
When referring to integers, the term **integral value** is used.
A number that is **non-integral** is not an integer.

Multiplying and dividing directed numbers

Multiply and divide the numbers as normal.
Then find the sign for the answer using these rules:
• two **like** signs (both + or both –) give a positive answer.
• two **unlike** signs (one + and the other –) give a negative answer.

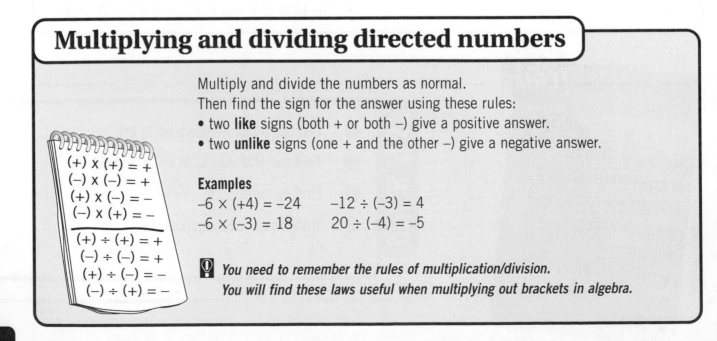

$(+) \times (+) = +$
$(-) \times (-) = +$
$(+) \times (-) = -$
$(-) \times (+) = -$

$(+) \div (+) = +$
$(-) \div (-) = +$
$(+) \div (-) = -$
$(-) \div (+) = -$

Examples

$-6 \times (+4) = -24$ $-12 \div (-3) = 4$
$-6 \times (-3) = 18$ $20 \div (-4) = -5$

You need to remember the rules of multiplication/division.
You will find these laws useful when multiplying out brackets in algebra.

Adding and subtracting directed numbers

Example

The temperature at 6 a.m. was –5°C. By 10 a.m. it had risen 8 degrees.
So the new temperature was 3°C.

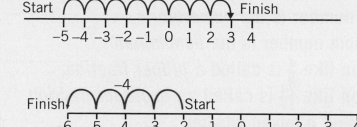

Example

Find the value of –2 – 4.

This represents the sign of
the number. Start at –2.

This represents the operation of
subtraction. Move 4 places to the left.

So –2 – 4 = –6.

- When the number to be added (or subtracted) is **negative**, the normal direction of movement is **reversed**.

Example

–4 – (–3) is the same as –4 + 3 = –1

  The negative changes the **direction**. Move 3 places to the **right**.

- When two (+) or two (–) signs are together, these rules are used:

$$\left. \begin{array}{l} +(+) \rightarrow + \\ -(-) \rightarrow + \end{array} \right\} \text{ like signs give a positive} \qquad \left. \begin{array}{l} +(-) \rightarrow - \\ -(+) \rightarrow - \end{array} \right\} \text{ unlike signs give a negative.}$$

Examples

$-6 + (-2) = -6 - 2 = -8$ $-2 - (+6) = -2 - 6 = -8$

$4 - (-3) = 4 + 3 = 7$ $9 + (-3) = 9 - 3 = 6$

💡 *If you find working with directed numbers difficult, sketch a quick number line to help you.*

Negative numbers on the calculator

The +/– or (–) key on the calculator gives a
negative number.

For example, to get –6, press 6 +/– or
(–) 6 .

Example

$-4 - (-2) = -2$

is keyed in the calculator like this:

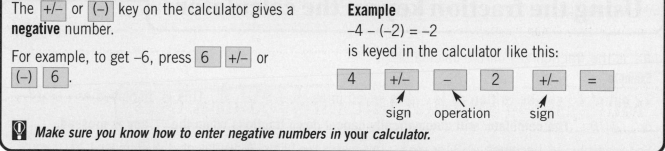

💡 *Make sure you know how to enter negative numbers in your calculator.*

KEY TERMS

Make sure you
understand these
terms before moving on!

- directed numbers
- integers

QUICK TEST

❶ If the temperature was –12°C at 2 a.m., and it rose by
15 degrees by 11 a.m., what was the temperature at
11 a.m.?

❷ Work these out, without a calculator.
 a) –2 – (–6) b) –9 + (–7) c) –2 × 6
 d) –9 + (–3) e) –20 ÷ (–4) f) –18 ÷ (–3)
 g) 4 – (–3) h) –7 + (–3) i) –9 × –4

Fractions

A fraction is a part of a whole.
The top number is the *numerator*.
The bottom number is the *denominator*.
A fraction like $\frac{4}{5}$ is called a *proper fraction*.
A fraction like $\frac{24}{17}$ is called an *improper fraction*.
$2\frac{1}{2}$ is called a mixed number.
$\frac{4}{5}$ means 4 parts out of 5.

When expressing one amount as a fraction of another amount, write them as a fraction with the first amount the numerator and the second the denominator. For example, 7 as a fraction of 9 is written as $\frac{7}{9}$.

Equivalent fractions

Equivalent fractions have the same value.

Example

$\frac{1}{2}$ $\frac{2}{4}$ $\frac{3}{6}$ $\frac{4}{8}$

From the diagrams it can be seen that
$\frac{1}{2} = \frac{2}{4} = \frac{3}{6} = \frac{4}{8}$.

They are equivalent fractions. Fractions can be changed to their equivalents by **multiplying** or **dividing** both the numerator and denominator by the same amount.

Examples

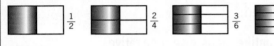

$\times 4$

$\frac{5}{7}$ $\frac{20}{28}$

$\times 4$

Change $\frac{5}{7}$ to its equivalent fraction with a denominator of 28.

• Multiply top and bottom by 4.

• So $\frac{5}{7}$ is equivalent to $\frac{20}{28}$.

$\div 20$

$\frac{40}{60}$ $\frac{2}{3}$

$\div 20$

Change $\frac{40}{60}$ to its equivalent fraction with a denominator of 3.

Divide top and bottom by 20.

So $\frac{40}{60}$ is equivalent to $\frac{2}{3}$.

This is known as simplifying the fraction by 'cancelling'.

Using the fraction key on the calculator

$\boxed{a\frac{b}{c}}$ is the fraction key on the calculator.

Example

12 out of 18 can be written as $\frac{12}{18}$. $\frac{12}{18}$ is keyed in as $\boxed{1}$ $\boxed{2}$ $\boxed{a\frac{b}{c}}$ $\boxed{1}$ $\boxed{8}$. This is displayed as $\boxed{12\lrcorner18}$

or $\boxed{12\ulcorner18}$. **The calculator will automatically cancel down fractions when the** $\boxed{=}$ **key is pressed.**

For example, $\frac{12}{18}$ becomes $\boxed{2\lrcorner3}$ or $\boxed{2\ulcorner3}$. This means two-thirds. A display of $\boxed{1\lrcorner4\lrcorner9}$ means $1\frac{4}{9}$. If you

now press $\boxed{\text{shift}}$ $\boxed{a\frac{b}{c}}$, it converts back to an improper fraction, $\boxed{13\lrcorner9}$ ($\frac{13}{9}$).

Multiplication and division of fractions

When multiplying and dividing fractions, write out whole or mixed numbers as improper fractions before starting.

Example

$1\frac{2}{9} \times \frac{4}{7} = \frac{11}{9} \times \frac{4}{7} = \frac{44}{63}$ ←—— Multiply numerators together.
←—— Multiply denominators together.

Change a division into a multiplication by turning the second fraction upside down and multiplying both fractions together; to divide by a fraction, **multiply by the reciprocal**.

Example

$\frac{7}{9} \div \frac{12}{18}$ Take the **reciprocal** of the second fraction.

$= \frac{7}{9} \times \frac{18}{12} = \frac{126}{108}$ Multiply fractions as normal

$= 1\frac{1}{6}$ Rewrite the answer as a mixed number.

Addition and subtraction of fractions

These examples show the basic principles of adding and subtracting fractions.

Example

$\frac{1}{8} + \frac{3}{4}$

- First make the denominators the same:

  $\frac{3}{4}$ is **equivalent** to $\frac{6}{8}$.

  $\frac{3}{4} \overset{\times 2}{\underset{\times 2}{=}} \frac{6}{8}$

$= \frac{1}{8} + \frac{6}{8}$

- Replace $\frac{3}{4}$ with $\frac{6}{8}$.

$= \frac{7}{8}$

- Add the numerators $1 + 6 = 7$.
  The denominator stays the same.

Example

$\frac{9}{12} - \frac{1}{3}$

- First make the denominators the same:

  $\frac{1}{3}$ is equivalent to $\frac{4}{12}$.

  $\frac{1}{3} \overset{\times 4}{\underset{\times 4}{=}} \frac{4}{12}$

$= \frac{9}{12} - \frac{4}{12}$

- Replace the $\frac{1}{3}$ with $\frac{4}{12}$.

$= \frac{5}{12}$

- Subtract the numerators but **not** the denominators;
  the denominator stays the same.

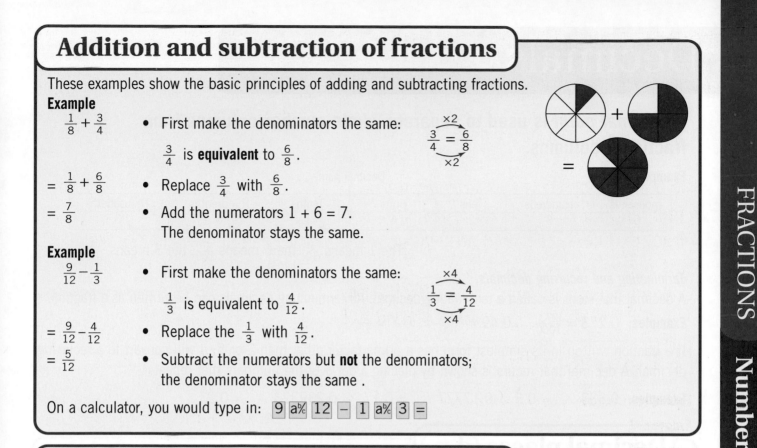

On a calculator, you would type in: $\boxed{9}\ \boxed{a\%}\ \boxed{12}\ \boxed{-}\ \boxed{1}\ \boxed{a\%}\ \boxed{3}\ \boxed{=}$

Proportional changes with fractions

Increase and decrease

There are two methods. Use the one that is familiar to you. Remember that 'of' means multiply.

Example

Last year a gym had 290 members.
This year there are $\frac{3}{5}$ more.
How many members are there now?

Method 1

$\frac{3}{5} \times 290 = 174$ Work out $\frac{3}{5}$ of 290.

$290 + 174 = 464$ people   Add this to the original number.

Method 2

Increasing by $\frac{3}{5}$ is the same as multiplying by $1\frac{3}{5}$

$(1 + \frac{3}{5})$:

$1\frac{3}{5} \times 290 = 464$

On the calculator, key in $\boxed{1}\ \boxed{a\%}\ \boxed{3}\ \boxed{a\%}\ \boxed{5}\ \boxed{x}\ \boxed{290}\ \boxed{=}$

💡 *Questions involving fractions are quite common on the non-calculator paper. Learn the quick way of finding a fraction of a quantity.*

KEY TERMS

Make sure you understand these terms before moving on!
- numerator
- denominator
- proper fraction
- improper fraction

QUICK TEST

❶ Without using a calculator, work out the following:

a) $\frac{2}{9} + \frac{3}{27}$ b) $\frac{3}{5} - \frac{1}{4}$ c) $\frac{6}{9} \times \frac{72}{104}$ d) $\frac{8}{9} \div \frac{2}{3}$

e) $\frac{4}{7} - \frac{1}{3}$ f) $\frac{2}{7} \div 1\frac{1}{2}$ g) $\frac{7}{11} \div \frac{22}{14}$ h) $\frac{2}{9} + \frac{4}{7}$

❷ Calculate $\frac{2}{9}$ of £180.

❸ $\frac{7}{12}$ more rain fell this year than last.
If 156 mm fell last year, how much fell this year?

Decimals

A *decimal point* is used to separate whole number columns from fractional columns.

Example

Decimal point

Thousands	Hundreds	Tens	Units		Tenths	Hundredths	Thousandths
5	9	2	4	.	1	6	3

The 1 means $\frac{1}{10}$, the 6 means $\frac{6}{100}$, the 3 means $\frac{3}{1000}$

Terminating and recurring decimals

A decimal that stops is called a terminating decimal. All terminating decimals can be written as a fraction.

Examples: $0.273 = \frac{273}{1000}$ $0.49 = \frac{49}{100}$ $0.7 = \frac{7}{10}$

If a fraction written in its simplest form has a prime factor other than 2 or 5, it will convert to a recurring decimal. A decimal that recurs is shown by placing a dot over the numbers that repeat.

Examples: $0.333 \ldots = 0.\dot{3}$ $0.17777 \ldots = 0.1\dot{7}$ $0.232323 \ldots = 0.\dot{2}\dot{3}$

Decimal places (d.p.)

When rounding numbers to a specified number of decimal places:

- look at the last number that is wanted (e.g. if rounding 12.367 to 2 d.p., look at the 6 which is in the second d.p.);
- look at the number to the right of it (the number which is not needed – i.e. the 7);

- if it is **5 or more**, then **round up the last digit** (7 is greater than 5, so round up the 6 to a 7);
- if it is **less than 5**, then the digit remains the **same**.

Examples

12.49 = 12.5 to 1 d.p.
8.735 = 8.74 to 2 d.p.
9.624 = 9.62 to 2 d.p.

Ordering decimals

When ordering decimals:

- First write them all with the same number of digits after the decimal point.
- Then compare whole numbers, digits in the tenths place, digits in the hundredths place, and so on.

Examples

Arrange these numbers in order of size, smallest first:

6.21, 6.023, 6.4, 6.04, 2.71, 9.4

First rewrite them:

6.210, 6.023, 6.400, 6.040, 2.710, 9.400

Then re-order them:

2.710, 6.023, 6.040, 6.210, 6.400, 9.400

Remember, hundredths are smaller than tenths: $\frac{10}{100} = \frac{1}{10}$ *so* $\frac{6}{100} < \frac{1}{10}$

Multiplying and dividing by numbers between 0 and 1

When **multiplying** by numbers between 0 and 1, the result is **smaller** than the starting value.
When **dividing** by numbers between 0 and 1, the result is **bigger** than the starting value.

Examples

$6 \times 0.1 = 0.6$
$6 \times 0.01 = 0.06$
$6 \times 0.001 = 0.006$

The results are all smaller than the starting values.

$6 \div 0.1 = 60$
$6 \div 0.01 = 600$
$6 \div 0.001 = 6000$

The results are all bigger than the starting values.

Calculations with decimals

When **adding** and **subtracting** decimals, align the decimal points in a column.

Examples

```
  27.46
   7.291 +
  34.751
   1  1
```

Line up the digits carefully.

Put the decimal points under each other.

```
    6 9 1
  1⁷.⁄00
  12.84 –
   4.16
```

The decimal point in the answer will be in line.

When **dividing** decimals, divide as normal, placing the decimal points in line.

Example

```
      4.8
  3 ⟌1 4.²4
```

Put the decimal points in line.

When **dividing by a decimal**, it makes it easier to multiply the numerator and denominator by a power of 10, so that it becomes equivalent to a division with a whole number.

Example

$$\frac{2.75}{0.25} = \frac{27500}{25}$$

Multiply numerator and denominator by 100.

$$= 1100$$

💡 *Multiplying and dividing by numbers between 0 and 1 usually occur on the non-calculator paper – it is wise to practise these by writing out several calculations and then checking your answers with a calculator.*

When **multiplying** decimals, the answer must have the same number of decimal places as the total number of decimal places in the numbers which are being multiplied.

Examples

Work out 24.6×7.

```
   246
     7 ×
  1722
   3 4
```

Multiply 246 by 7 = 1722, ignoring the decimal point. 24.6 has 1 digit after the decimal point. The answer must have 1 decimal place (1 d.p.).

So $24.6 \times 7 = 172.2$

Work out 4.52×0.2

```
   452
     2 ×
   904
     1
```

Work out 452×2, ignoring the decimal points.
4.52 has 2 d.p.; 0.2 has 1 d.p.
So the answer must have 3 d.p.

$904 \rightarrow 0.904$ Move the digits 3 places to the right.
So $4.52 \times 0.2 = 0.904$

Example

Change $\frac{3}{5}$ into a decimal by short division.

```
      0.6
  5 ⟌3.³0
```

QUICK TEST

❶ Without using a calculator, work out the following.
   a) 27.16 + 9.32   b) 29.04 – 11.361   c) 12.8 × 2.1
   d) 49.2 ÷ 4   e) 600 × 0.01   f) 520 × 0.1
   g) 20 × 0.02   h) 37 × 0.0001   i) 400 ÷ 0.1
   j) 450 ÷ 0.01   k) 470 ÷ 0.001   l) 650 ÷ 0.02

❷ Round the following numbers to 2 decimal places.
   a) 7.469
   b) 12.0372
   c) 9.365
   d) 10.042
   e) 8.1794

Percentages 1

Percentages are fractions with a denominator of 100.
% is the percentage sign.
75% means $\frac{75}{100}$ (this is also equal to $\frac{3}{4}$).

75%

Percentage of a quantity

Again, the word '**of**' means **multiply**.

Example

40% of £600 becomes

$\frac{40}{100} \times 600 = £240$

On the calculator, key in

40 ÷ 100 x 600 =

If this is on the non-calculator paper:

- Work out 10% first by dividing by 10
  600 ÷10 = £60
- Multiply by 4 to get 40%
  4 × 60 = £240

Percentage questions appear frequently at GCSE. If there is a percentage question on the non-calculator paper, first work out what 10% is equal to, as shown in the example above.

Example

A meal for four costs £92.20.
VAT (value added tax) is charged at 17.5%.
a) How much VAT is there to pay on the meal?
b) What is the final price of the meal?

a) 17.5% of £92.20 = $\frac{17.5}{100} \times 92.20$
$= £16.14$ to the nearest penny
VAT = £16.14

b) Price of meal = £92.20 + £16.14 = £108.34

An alternative is to use a **scale factor method**:
An increase of 17.5%, is the same as multiplying
by 1.175 = 1 + $\frac{17.5}{100}$.

£92.20 × 1.175
= £108.34 (to the nearest penny)

Percentage increase and decrease

The answers to these questions will be a percentage so multiply the change by 100%.

$$\% \text{ change} = \frac{\text{change}}{\text{original}} \times 100\%$$

Example

A coat costs £125.
In a sale it is reduced to £85.
What is the percentage reduction?

Reduction = £125 – £85 = £40

% reduction = $\frac{40}{125} \times 100\%$

$= 32\%$

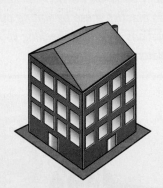
~~£125~~ £85

Example

Matthew bought a flat for £145 000.
Three years later, he sold it for £162 000.
What was his percentage profit?

Profit = £162 000 – £145 000
= £17 000

% Profit = $\frac{17000}{145000} \times 100\%$

= 11.72%

12

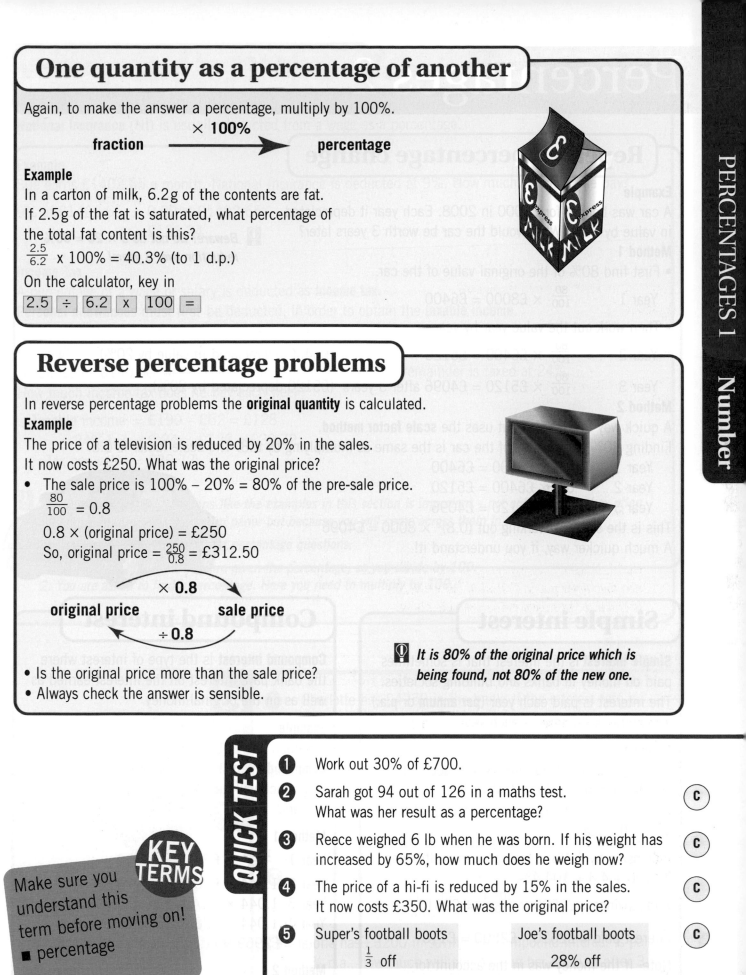

One quantity as a percentage of another

Again, to make the answer a percentage, multiply by 100%.

fraction → (× 100%) → percentage

Example
In a carton of milk, 6.2g of the contents are fat.
If 2.5g of the fat is saturated, what percentage of
the total fat content is this?
$\frac{2.5}{6.2}$ × 100% = 40.3% (to 1 d.p.)

On the calculator, key in
[2.5] [÷] [6.2] [x] [100] [=]

Reverse percentage problems

In reverse percentage problems the **original quantity** is calculated.
Example
The price of a television is reduced by 20% in the sales.
It now costs £250. What was the original price?

- The sale price is 100% − 20% = 80% of the pre-sale price.
  $\frac{80}{100}$ = 0.8

  0.8 × (original price) = £250
  So, original price = $\frac{250}{0.8}$ = £312.50

original price ⟷ (× 0.8 / ÷ 0.8) ⟷ sale price

💡 *It is 80% of the original price which is being found, not 80% of the new one.*

- Is the original price more than the sale price?
- Always check the answer is sensible.

KEY TERMS
Make sure you understand this term before moving on!
■ percentage

QUICK TEST

1. Work out 30% of £700.

2. Sarah got 94 out of 126 in a maths test. What was her result as a percentage? (C)

3. Reece weighed 6 lb when he was born. If his weight has increased by 65%, how much does he weigh now? (C)

4. The price of a hi-fi is reduced by 15% in the sales. It now costs £350. What was the original price? (C)

5. Super's football boots $\frac{1}{3}$ off   Joe's football boots 28% off (C)

   If a pair of football boots costs £49.99, which shop is selling them cheaper in the sale and what is their price?

   (C) *Indicates that a calculator may be used.*

Equivalents

Fractions to decimals to percentages

Equivalent fractions, decimals and percentages are all different ways of expressing the same number.

The table opposite shows:
- Some common fractions and their **equivalents** which you need to learn
- How to convert fractions ➡ decimals ➡ percentages

💡 *Get a friend to test you on the equivalences between fractions, decimals and percentages. You need to learn all the ones in the table.*

Fraction	Decimal	Percentage
$\frac{1}{2}$	0.5	50%
$\frac{1}{3}$	0.3̇3̇	33.3̇%
$\frac{2}{3}$	0.66̇	66.6̇%
$\frac{1}{4}$	0.25	25%
$\frac{3}{4}$	3 ÷ 4 ➡ 0.75 ✕ 100% 75%
$\frac{1}{5}$	0.2	20%
$\frac{1}{8}$	0.125	12.5%
$\frac{3}{8}$	0.375	37.5%
$\frac{1}{10}$	0.1	10%
$\frac{1}{100}$	0.01	1%

Ordering fractions

When ordering fractions it is useful to write them with a common denominator so that you can compare the numerators.

Example

Place these fractions in order of size, smallest first. $\frac{1}{4}, \frac{3}{10}, \frac{5}{8}, \frac{7}{20}, \frac{27}{40}$

Since all the fractions can be rewritten with a denominator of 40, we can compare the numerators.
$\frac{10}{40}, \frac{12}{40}, \frac{25}{40}, \frac{14}{40}, \frac{27}{40}$

In size order: $\frac{10}{40}, \frac{12}{40}, \frac{14}{40}, \frac{25}{40}, \frac{27}{40} = \frac{1}{4}, \frac{3}{10}, \frac{7}{20}, \frac{5}{8}, \frac{27}{40}$

Ordering different numbers

When putting a mixture of fractions, decimals and percentages in order of size, it is best to change them all to decimals first.

Example

$\frac{3}{5}$, 0.65, 0.273, 27%, 62%, $\frac{4}{9}$

0.6, 0.65, 0.273, 0.27, 0.62, 0.4̇4̇   Put into decimals first.

0.27, 0.273, 0.4̇4̇, 0.6, 0.62, 0.65   Place in order of size, smallest first.

27%, 0.273, $\frac{4}{9}$, $\frac{3}{5}$, 62%, 0.65

---

❶ Change the following fractions into a) decimals b) percentages
   i) $\frac{2}{7}$ ii) $\frac{3}{5}$ iii) $\frac{8}{9}$ Ⓒ

❷ Place the following in order of size, smallest first.
   $\frac{2}{5}$, 0.42, 0.041, $\frac{1}{3}$, 5%, 26%

   Ⓒ *Indicates that a calculator may be used.*

QUICK TEST

 Make sure you understand this term before moving on!
■ equivalents
KEY TERMS

Using a calculator

Order of operations

BIDMAS is a made-up word which helps you to remember the order in which calculations take place.

B   I   D   M   A   S

Brackets   Indices   Division   Multiplication   Addition   Subtraction

This just means anything in brackets is done first, then the other operations are done in this order.

Examples

$(2 + 4) \times 3 = 18$ but $2 + 4 \times 3 = 14$, *not* 18, because without the brackets the multiplication is done first.

Important calculator keys

Make sure you are familiar with the keys on your own calculator.

Shift or 2nd or Inv allow 2nd functions to be carried out

allows a fraction to be put in the calculator

− or +/− changes positive numbers to negative ones

bracket keys

often puts the ×10 part in when working in standard form

pressing shift or EXP often gives π

square root

square

trigonometric buttons

memory keys

works out powers

cancels only the last key you have pressed

memory key

A calculator display of 4^{07} means 4×10^7

Calculating powers

y^x or x^y is used for calculating powers, e.g. 2^7.
- Use the power key on the calculator to work out 2^7.
- Write down calculator keys used.
- Check that you obtain the answer 128.

Now try writing down the keys that would be needed for these calculations.

Check that you get the right answers.

a) $\frac{2.9 \times 3.6}{(4.2 + 3.7)} = 1.322$ b) $9^{\frac{1}{3}} \times 4^5 = 2130$ c) $\frac{3 \times (5.2)^2}{9.6 \times (12.4)^3} = 4.432 \times 10^{-3}$

QUICK TEST

❶   Work out these on your calculator: Ⓒ

a) $\frac{27.1 \times 6.4}{9.3 + 2.7}$ b) $\frac{(9.3)^4}{2.7 \times 3.6}$

c) $\sqrt{\frac{25^2}{4\pi}}$ d) $\frac{5}{9}(25 - 10)$

Ⓒ   *Indicates that a calculator may be used.*

Approximating and checking calculations

Significant figures (s.f. or sig. fig.)

The 1st **significant figure** is the first digit which is not zero. The 2nd, 3rd, 4th, ... significant figures follow on after the 1st digit. They may or may not be zeros.

Examples

      6 . 4 0 2 7 has 5 s.f.   0 . 0 0 0 4 7 0 1 has 4 s.f.

      1st 2nd 3rd 4th 5th   1st 2nd 3rd 4th

To round a number to a given number of significant places, apply the same rule as with decimal places: if the next digit is 5 or more, round up.

Examples

Number	to 3 s.f.	to 2 s.f.	to 1 s.f.
4.207	4.21	4.2	4
4379	4380	4400	4000
0.006209	0.00621	0.0062	0.006

After rounding the last digit, you must fill in the end zeros. For example, 4380 = 4400 to 2 s.f. (not 44).

Take care when rounding that you do not change the place values.

Estimates and approximations

Estimating is a good way of checking answers.
- Round the numbers to 'easy' numbers, usually ones with 1 or 2 significant figures.
- Work out the estimate using these easy numbers.
- Use the symbol ≈, which means '**approximately equal to**'.
- For multiplying or dividing, never approximate a number to zero. Use 0.1, 0.01, 0.001, etc.

Examples

a) $8.93 \times 25.09 \approx 10 \times 25 = 250$ b) $(6.29)^2 \approx 6^2 = 36$

c) $\frac{296 \times 52.1}{9.72 \times 1.14} \approx \frac{300 \times 50}{10 \times 1} = \frac{15000}{10} = 1500$ d) $0.096 \times 79.2 \approx 0.1 \times 80 = 8$

Example

Jack does the calculation $\frac{9.6 \times 103}{(2.9)^2}$

a) Estimate the answer to this calculation, without using a calculator.

b) Jack's answer is 1175.7. Is this the **right order of magnitude** (about the right size)?

a) Estimate: $\frac{9.6 \times 103}{(2.9)^2} \approx \frac{10 \times 100}{3^2} = \frac{1000}{9} \approx \frac{1000}{10} = 100$

b) Jack's answer is not the right order of magnitude. It is 10 times too big.

- When adding and subtracting, very small numbers may be approximated to zero.

Examples

$109.6 + 0.0002 \approx 110 + 0 = 110$ $63.87 - 0.01 \approx 64 - 0 = 64$

Questions which involve approximating are common on the non-calculator paper. For most of these questions, you are expected to round to 1 significant figure. Even if you find the calculation difficult, show your approximations to pick up method marks.

Checking calculations

When checking calculations, the process used can be reversed.

Examples

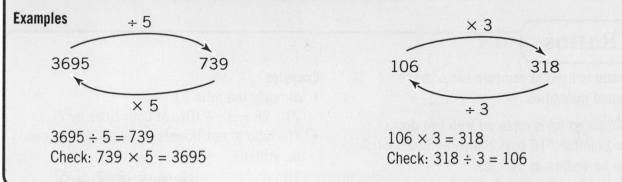

$\div 5$

3695 → 739

$\times 5$

$3695 \div 5 = 739$
Check: $739 \times 5 = 3695$

$\times 3$

106 → 318

$\div 3$

$106 \times 3 = 318$
Check: $318 \div 3 = 106$

Calculations

When solving problems the answers should be rounded sensibly.

Example

$95.26 \times 6.39 = 608.7114 = 608.71$ (2 d.p.)

Round to 2 d.p. because the values in the question are to 2 d.p.

When rounding remainders, consider the context of the question.

Example

Jackie has £9.37. She divides it equally between 5 people. How much does each person receive?

$£9.37 \div 5 = £1.874$
$\qquad\qquad = £1.87$
(Round to 2 d.p. as it is money.)

Example

Paint is sold in 8 litre tins. Sandra needs 27 litres of paint. How many tins must she buy?

$27 \div 8 = 3$ remainder 3

Sandra needs 4 tins of paint.
Sandra would not have enough paint with 3 tins – she would be 3 litres short. Hence, the number of tins of paint must be rounded up.

You will lose marks if you do not write money to 2 d.p. If the answer to a money calculation is £9.7, always write it to 2 d.p. i.e. £9.70.

KEY TERMS

Make sure you understand this term before moving on!
■ significant figure

QUICK TEST

1. Round the following numbers to 3 significant figures (3 s.f.)
   a) 0.003786   b) 27 490   c) 307 250

2. Estimate the answer to $\frac{(29.4)^2 + 106}{2.2 \times 5.1}$

3. Sukhvinder decided to decorate her living room. The total area of the walls was 48 m². If one roll of wallpaper covers 5 m² of wall, how many rolls of wallpaper did Sukhvinder need?   (C)

4. Thomas earned £109.25 for working a 23-hour week. How much was he paid per hour? Check your calculation by estimating.

(C) *Indicates that a calculator may be used.*

Ratio

Ratios

- A **ratio** is used to compare two or more related quantities.

- 'Compared to' is replaced with two dots **:**
  For example, '16 boys compared to 20 girls' can be written as 16 : 20.

- To simplify ratios, divide both parts of the ratio by their highest common factor.
  For example, 16 : 20 = 4 : 5
  (Divide both sides by 4.)

Examples
- Simplify the ratio 21 : 28.
  21 : 28 = 3 : 4 (Divide both sides by 7)
- The ratio of red flowers to yellow flowers can be written:
  10 : 4
  = 5 : 2

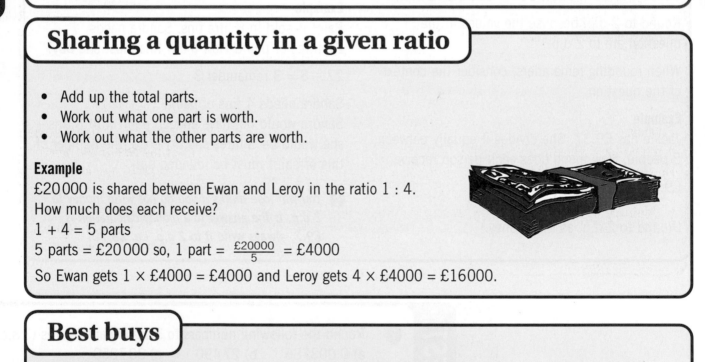

In other words, for every 5 red flowers there are 2 yellow flowers.
To express the ratio 5 : 2 as the ratio n : 1, divide both sides by 2:
$$5 : 2 = \frac{5}{2} : \frac{2}{2}$$
$$= 2.5 : 1$$

Sharing a quantity in a given ratio

- Add up the total parts.
- Work out what one part is worth.
- Work out what the other parts are worth.

Example
£20 000 is shared between Ewan and Leroy in the ratio 1 : 4.
How much does each receive?
1 + 4 = 5 parts
5 parts = £20 000 so, 1 part = $\frac{£20000}{5}$ = £4000

So Ewan gets 1 × £4000 = £4000 and Leroy gets 4 × £4000 = £16 000.

Best buys

Use unit amounts to decide which option is the better value for money.

Example
The same brand of coffee is sold in two different-sized jars.
Which jar represents the better value for money?

- Find the cost per gram for both jars.

  100 g costs 186 p so 186 ÷ 100 = 1.86 p per gram.
  250 g costs 247 p so 247 ÷ 250 = 0.988 p per gram.

Since the larger jar costs less per gram it offers the better value for money.

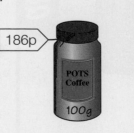

Increasing and decreasing in a given ratio

- Divide to get one part.
- Multiply for each new part.

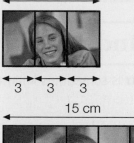

9 cm

15 cm

Example

A photograph of length 9 cm is to be enlarged in the ratio 5 : 3.
What is the length of the enlarged photograph?

- Divide 9 cm by 3 to get 1 part.
  $9 \div 3 = 3$
- Multiply this by 5.
  $5 \times 3 = 15$ cm

So the length 9 cm is 15 cm on the enlarged photograph.

Example

A house took 8 people 6 days to build.
At the same rate, how long would it take 3 people?
Time for 8 people = 6 days
Time for 1 person = $8 \times 6 = 48$ days
It takes 1 person longer to build the house.
So time for 3 people = $\frac{48}{3} = 16$ days
3 people will take $\frac{1}{3}$ of the time taken by 1 person.

Example

A recipe for 4 people needs 1600 g of flour.
How much is needed to make the recipe for 6 people?
- Divide 1600 g by 4: 400 g for 1 person.
- Multiply by 6, so 6×400 g = 2400 g for 6 people.

FLOUR

> **When answering problems of the type shown here, always try and work out what a unit (or one) is worth. You should then be able to work out what any other value is worth.**

RATIO   Number

QUICK TEST

1. Write the following ratios in their simplest form:

   a) 12 : 15
   b) 6 : 12
   c) 25 : 10

2. Three sisters share 60 sweets between them in the ratio 2 : 3 : 7. How many sweets does each sister receive?

3. If 15 oranges cost £1.80, how much will 23 identical oranges cost?

4. A map is being enlarged in the ratio 12 : 7. If a road length was 21 cm on the original map, what is the length of the road on the enlarged map?

Indices

Indices

An **index** is sometimes known as a **power**.

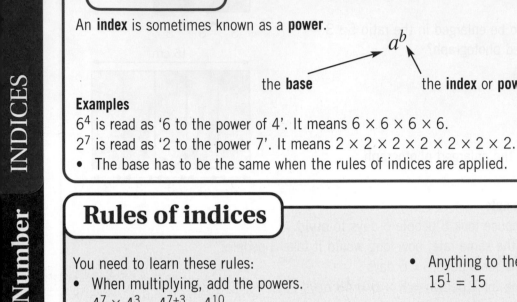

$$a^b$$

the **base**   the **index** or **power**

Examples

6^4 is read as '6 to the power of 4'. It means $6 \times 6 \times 6 \times 6$.

2^7 is read as '2 to the power 7'. It means $2 \times 2 \times 2 \times 2 \times 2 \times 2 \times 2$.

• The base has to be the same when the rules of indices are applied.

Rules of indices

You need to learn these rules:

• When multiplying, add the powers.
$$4^7 \times 4^3 = 4^{7+3} = 4^{10}$$

• When dividing, subtract the powers.
$$6^9 \div 6^4 = 6^{9-4} = 6^5$$

• When raising one power to another, multiply the powers.
$$(7^2)^4 = 7^{2\times4} = 7^8$$

• Anything raised to the **power zero** is **1**, provided the number is not zero.
$$5^0 = 1 \qquad 6^0 = 1$$
$$2.7189^0 = 1 \qquad 0^0 = \text{undefined}$$

• Anything to the **power 1** is **itself**.
$$15^1 = 15 \qquad 1923^1 = 1923$$

• All these rules also apply when the powers are negative.

Examples
$$6^{-2} \times 6^{12} = 6^{-2+12} = 6^{10}$$
$$8^{-4} \times 8^{-3} = 8^{-4+-3} = 8^{-7}$$
$$(6^4)^{-2} = 6^{4 \times -2} = 6^{-8}$$
$$5^0 = 1$$

Negative and fractional powers

At GCSE Higher level there are a few more properties of indices that need to be learnt:

Negative powers

Turn a negative power **upside down** (take the reciprocal) to make the **power positive**.

In general, $a^{-n} = \frac{1}{a^n}$.

Examples
$$4^{-2} = \frac{1}{4^2} = \frac{1}{16} \qquad \left(\frac{2}{3}\right)^{-2} = \left(\frac{3}{2}\right)^2 = \frac{9}{4} \qquad 2x^{-3} = \frac{2}{x^3}$$

Fractional powers

These mean **roots**!

In general, $a^{\frac{1}{m}} = \sqrt[m]{a}$.

• The power $\frac{1}{2}$ means square root $\sqrt{}$.

• The power $\frac{1}{3}$ means cube root $\sqrt[3]{}$.

• The power $\frac{1}{4}$ means fourth root $\sqrt[4]{}$, etc.

Examples
$$25^{\frac{1}{2}} = \sqrt{25} = 5 \qquad 8^{\frac{1}{3}} = \sqrt[3]{8} = 2$$
$$81^{\frac{1}{4}} = \sqrt[4]{81} = 3$$

Sometimes powers are written as fractions.

In general, $a^{\frac{n}{m}} = (\sqrt[m]{a})^n$.

Examples
$$8^{\frac{2}{3}} = (\sqrt[3]{8})^2 = 2^2 = 4$$
$$64^{\frac{5}{6}} = (\sqrt[6]{64})^5 = 2^5 = 32$$

If there is a negative fraction, remember to turn it upside down as well (take the reciprocal).

$$125^{-\frac{2}{3}} = \frac{1}{125^{\frac{2}{3}}} = \frac{1}{(\sqrt[3]{125})^2} = \frac{1}{5^2} = \frac{1}{25}$$

$$(2x)^{-3} = \frac{1}{(2x)^3} = \frac{1}{8x^3}$$

Indices and algebra

The rules that apply with numbers also apply with algebra.

Laws of indices

$$a^n \times a^m = a^{n+m}$$

$$a^n \div a^m = a^{n-m}$$

$$(a^n)^m = a^{n \times m}$$

$$a^0 = 1$$

$$a^1 = a$$

$$a^{-n} = \frac{1}{a^n}$$

$$a^{\frac{1}{m}} = \sqrt[m]{a}$$

Indices are a very common topic on the non-calculator paper – learn the rules and you should be OK!

Examples

Note that the numbers are multiplied ...

$$4x^2 \times 3x^5 = 12x^7$$

$$12x^4 \div 3x^7 = 4x^{-3}$$

... but the powers of the same letter are added

$$(7x^2)^2 = 49x^4$$

$$x^0 = 1$$

$$(2x^4)^3 = 8x^{12}$$

Simplify the following expressions:

$$\frac{3x^7 \times 4x^9}{6x^4} = \frac{12x^{16}}{6x^4} = 2x^{12}$$

Work this out in 2 stages.

$$x^6 \times 4x^3 = 4x^9$$

$$\frac{12a^2b^3}{6a^3b^2} = \frac{2b}{a}$$

$$\frac{4a^4b^3}{2ab} = 2a^3b^2$$

KEY TERMS

Make sure you understand these terms before moving on!

- index
- power
- base

QUICK TEST

1 Simplify the following:
a) $12^4 \times 12^8$ b) $9^{-2} \times 9^{-4}$ c) 4^0
d) $18^6 \div 18^{-2}$ e) $(4^2)^5$ f) 1^{20}

2 Simplify the following:
a) $x^4 \times x^9$ b) $2x^6 \times 3x^7$ c) $12x^4 \div 3x^2$
d) $25x^9 \div 5x^{-2}$ e) $\dfrac{5x^6 \times 4x^9}{10x^3}$

3 Evaluate:
a) $(64)^{\frac{2}{3}}$ b) 5^{-3} c) $144^{\frac{1}{2}}$ d) $36^{-\frac{1}{2}}$

4 Simplify:
a) $(4x)^{-2}$ b) $(6x^2y^4)^{-2}$

Standard index form (Standard form)

Standard index form

Standard index form is used to write very large numbers or very small numbers in a simpler way. When written in **standard form**, a number will be written as:

$$a \times 10^n$$

a must be at least 1 but not greater than 10, i.e. $1 \leqslant a < 10$.
n is the power of 10 by which you multiply (if n is positive), or divide (if n is negative).

Learn these rules:
- The number (a) must always be at least 1 but less than 10.
- The power of 10, n:
    If the number is big, n is positive.
    If the number is small, n is negative.

Big numbers

Examples
- Write 6 230 000 in standard form.

  Place the decimal point between the 6 and 2 to give
  6.230 000 ($1 \leqslant 6.23 < 10$).

  Work out how many times you multiply by 10 to restore the number.

  6 2 3 0 0 0 0   ($n = 6$)

  In standard form, 6 230 000 = 6.23×10^6

- 4371 = 4.371×10^3 in standard form.

Small numbers

Examples
- Write 0.003 71 in standard form.

  Place the decimal point between the 3 and 7 to give 3.71 ($1 \leqslant 3.71 < 10$).

  Work out how many times you divide the number by 10.

  0 . 0 0 3 7 1   ($n = 3$)

  In standard form, 0.00371 = 3.71×10^{-3}

- 0.000 047 9 = 4.79×10^{-5} in standard form.

Standard form and the calculator

To key a number in standard form into the calculator, use the EXP key.
(Some calculators use EE . Make sure that you check your calculator, as calculators vary greatly.)

Examples

6.23×10^6 can be keyed in as: 6 . 2 3 EXP 6

4.93×10^{-5} can be keyed in as: 4 . 9 3 EXP 5 +/–

Most calculators do not show standard form correctly on the display.

7.632⁰⁹ means 7.632×10^9.   4.62⁻⁰⁷ means 4.62×10^{-7}.

Remember to put in the '× 10' part if the sign has been left out.

Calculations with standard form

You can use the calculator to do complex calculations in standard form.

It is important that you know how your calculator works

Examples

$(2.6 \times 10^3) \times (8.9 \times 10^{12}) = 2.314 \times 10^{16}$

This would be keyed in as:

| 2 | . | 6 | EXP | 3 | X | 8 | . | 9 | EXP | 1 | 2 | = |

Check that for $(1.8 \times 10^6) \div (2.7 \times 10^{-3})$
the answer is 6.7×10^8.

Just key in as normal:

| 2 | . | 7 | EXP | +/– | 3 |

If a calculation with standard form is on the
non-calculator paper, the laws of indices can be used when multiplying and dividing
numbers written in standard form.

Examples

$(2.4 \times 10^{-4}) \times (3 \times 10^7)$ $\qquad$ $(12.4 \times 10^{-4}) \div (4 \times 10^7)$

$= (2.4 \times 3) \times (10^{-4} \times 10^7)$ $\qquad$ $= (12.4 \div 4) \times (10^{-4} \div 10^7)$

$= 7.2 \times 10^3$ $\qquad\qquad\qquad$ $= 3.1 \times 10^{-11}$

Standard form questions are very common on both the calculator and non-calculator paper.

Watch out!

Several common mistakes when answering standard form questions are:

- *Reading a calculator display* $\boxed{2.4^{07}}$ *incorrectly and writing down 2.4⁷ instead of 2.4×10^7.*

- *Forgetting to write the answer in standard form, particularly on the non-calculator paper.*

  e.g. $(2 \times 10^6) \times (6 \times 10^3) = (2 \times 6) \times (10^6 \times 10^3)$

  $\qquad\qquad\qquad\qquad\qquad = 12 \times 10^9$

  $\qquad\qquad\qquad\qquad\qquad = 1.2 \times 10^{10}$

QUICK TEST

1 Write the following numbers in standard form:
   a) 630 000 b) 2730 c) 0.000 042 9 d) 0.000 000 63

2 Without a calculator work out the following, leaving your answers in standard form.
   a) $(2 \times 10^5) \times (3 \times 10^7)$ $\qquad$ b) $(6.1 \times 10^{12}) \times (2 \times 10^{-4})$
   c) $(8 \times 10^9) \div (2 \times 10^6)$ $\qquad$ d) $(6 \times 10^8) \div (2 \times 10^{-10})$

3 Work these out on a calculator. Give your answers to 3 s.f. **C**
   a) $\dfrac{1.279 \times 10^9}{2.94 \times 10^{-2}}$ $\qquad$ b) $(1.693 \times 10^4) \times (2.71 \times 10^{12})$

4 Calculate, giving your answer in standard form correct to 3 s.f. **C**
   $\dfrac{(3.72 \times 10^8) - (1.6 \times 10^4)}{3.81 \times 10^{-3}}$

C *Indicates that a calculator may be used.*

Direct and inverse proportion

The notation ∝ means 'is directly proportional to'. This is often abbreviated to 'is proportional to'. For example, $y \propto x^3$ is read as 'y is proportional to x cubed'.

Direct proportion

$y \propto x$ means that when x is multiplied by a number, then so is the corresponding value of y.

Example

x	2	4	12	48
y	3	6	18	72

×2 ×3 ×4

For **direct proportion**, the graph of y against x goes through the origin. For $y \propto x$, the graph is a straight line through the origin.

$y \propto x$

Inverse proportion

$y \propto \frac{1}{x}$ means that y is **inversely proportional** to x: when x is multiplied by a number, then y is divided by that number, and vice versa.

Example

x	4	16	48	24
y	12	3	1	2

×4 ×3 ÷2
÷4 ÷3 ×2

For **inverse proportion**, the graphs of y against x go to infinity when x or $y = 0$.
The graph of $y = \frac{1}{x}$ looks like this:

$y = \frac{1}{x}$

Variation

These are common GCSE questions that usually involve statements such as:

'a is proportional to the square of b'
'c is proportional to the square root of d'
'p is inversely proportional to a^2'
'd varies as the square of x'

Example
The value (V) of a diamond varies directly with the square of its weight (w).
A diamond weighing 5.0g is worth £2500.
How heavy is a diamond that is worth £6000?

Step 1 Change the sentence into a proportionality expression using the symbol ∝: $V \propto w^2$
Step 2 Replace ∝ with '$= k$' to make an equation:
  $V = kw^2$
Step 3 Substitute the values given in the question in order to find k: $2500 = k \times 5^2$
Step 4 Rearrange the equation to find the value of k.
  $\frac{2500}{5^2} = k \therefore k = 100$

Step 5 Put the value of k back into the equation:
  $V = 100w^2$
Step 6 Now answer the question using the equation you have found.
  $6000 = 100 \times w^2$
  $\frac{6000}{100} = w^2$
  $w = \sqrt{60}$
  $w = 7.75g$ (2 d.p.)

You use exactly the same steps if y is inversely proportional to x, except the equation in Step 2 would be $y = \frac{k}{x}$.

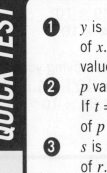

QUICK TEST

1. y is inversely proportional to the square of x. If $x = 5$ when $y = 4$, work out the value of y when $x = 10$.
2. p varies as the square root of t. If $t = 16$ when $p = 12$, find the value of p when $t = 49$.
3. s is inversely proportional to the cube of r. If $r = 2$ when $s = 5$, what is the value of r when $s = 10$?

Recurring decimals and surds

Changing recurring decimals into fractions

As **recurring decimals** are rational numbers, we can change them to fractions.

Example

Change $0.\dot{1}\dot{3}$ to a fraction in its lowest terms.

Let $x = 0.131313...$ (1)
then $100x = 13.131313...$ (2)
(Multiply by 10^n, where n is the length of the recurring pattern. In this example it is 2.)

Subtract equation (1) from equation (2).

    $99x = 13$

This has the effect of making the recurring pattern disappear.

Divide to leave x.

    $x = \frac{13}{99}$

Since 13 is a prime number, this fraction is in its lowest terms.

    So $0.\dot{1}\dot{3} = \frac{13}{99}$.

'Trick' method

There is a quick method of changing recurring decimals to fractions – the fraction has the repeating unit on the top and the same number of nines on the bottom.

Examples

$0.\dot{2} = \frac{2}{9}$ $0.\dot{4}\dot{1} = \frac{41}{99}$ $0.\dot{1}\dot{2}\dot{3} = \frac{123}{999}$

$0.\dot{2}7\dot{1}\dot{3} = \frac{2713}{9999}$

Remember to simplify if possible.

If you have a question where there is one or more numbers that are not repeated, extra care is needed.

Example

Change $0.2\dot{3}$ into a fraction.

    $x = 0.2333...$ (1)
    $10x = 2.3333...$ (2) multiply by 10
    $100x = 23.3333...$ (3) multiply by 100

Subtract equation (2) from equation (3).

    $90x = 21$ $x = \frac{21}{90} = \frac{7}{30}$

Surds

Numbers written under a square root sign are called **surds** – $\sqrt{2}$, $\sqrt{3}$, $\sqrt{13}$ etc. Surds are **irrational numbers** because they cannot be written as fractions.

To work with surds, there are a few rules you need to learn.

- $\sqrt{a} \times \sqrt{b} = \sqrt{ab}$

Example $\sqrt{3} \times \sqrt{5} = \sqrt{15}$

- $(\sqrt{b})^2 = \sqrt{b} \times \sqrt{b} = b$

Example $(\sqrt{3})^2 = 3$

- $\frac{\sqrt{a}}{\sqrt{b}} = \sqrt{\frac{a}{b}}$

Example $\frac{\sqrt{10}}{\sqrt{2}} = \sqrt{\frac{10}{2}} = \sqrt{5}$

- $(a + \sqrt{b})^2 = (a + \sqrt{b})(a + \sqrt{b})$
  $= a^2 + 2a\sqrt{b} + (\sqrt{b})^2 = a^2 + 2a\sqrt{b} + b$

- $(a + \sqrt{b})(a - \sqrt{b})$
  $= a^2 - a\sqrt{b} + a\sqrt{b} - (\sqrt{b})^2 = a^2 - b$

Examples

Simplify $\sqrt{200}$.
(Hint – look for square factors.)
$\sqrt{200} = \sqrt{2} \times \sqrt{100}$
       $= 10 \times \sqrt{2}$
       $= 10\sqrt{2}$

Simplify $(\sqrt{2} + 3)(\sqrt{2} + 3)$.
$= (\sqrt{2})^2 + 3\sqrt{2} + 3\sqrt{2} + 9$
$= 2 + 6\sqrt{2} + 9$
$= 11 + 6\sqrt{2}$

Simplify $\frac{1}{\sqrt{5}}$.
Multiply the top and bottom by $\sqrt{5}$.
$\frac{1}{\sqrt{5}} \times \frac{\sqrt{5}}{\sqrt{5}} = \frac{\sqrt{5}}{5}$

This is known as '**rationalising the denominator**'.

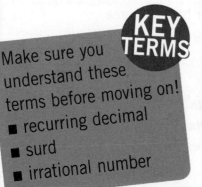

KEY TERMS

Make sure you understand these terms before moving on!

- recurring decimal
- surd
- irrational number

QUICK TEST

1. Change the following recurring decimals into fractions. Write them in their simplest form.
   a) $0.\dot{1}\dot{5}$ b) $0.\dot{7}$ c) $0.28\dot{3}$

2. Simplify the following:
   a) $\sqrt{75}$ b) $\sqrt{500}$ c) $(\sqrt{2} - 3)^2$
   d) $6(\sqrt{2} + 3) - \sqrt{2}(2 + \sqrt{3})$

3. Simplify $\frac{1}{\sqrt{3}}$

Upper and lower bounds of measurement

Upper and lower bounds for a single measurement

If a length x (cm) is given as 6.2, correct to the nearest millimetre, then by the usual conventions of rounding:

$$6.15 \leqslant x < 6.25$$

6.15 is called
the **lower bound**

6.25 is called
the **upper bound**

In general, the real value can be as much as half the unit above and below the rounded value.

Examples

If $x = 6.23$ (correct to 2 d.p.) then the rounded unit is 0.01, so the real value can be anything between $6.225 \leqslant 6.23 < 6.235$

Finding the maximum and minimum possible values of a calculation

When calculations are carried out using rounded values, then the calculated value lies between a maximum and minimum possible value.

Example 1

A desk measures 62 cm by 95 cm. Work out the lower and upper bounds of the area of the desk.

lower bound

upper bound

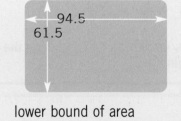

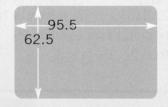

lower bound of area
= 61.5 × 94.5 = 5811.75 cm²

upper bound of area
= 62.5 × 95.5 = 5968.75 cm²

The rounded value = 95 × 62 = 5890 cm²

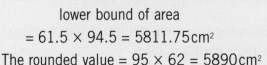 *This is a popular topic on exam papers. You must be careful on questions with division and subtraction, as it is easy to make a mistake. If in doubt, try all the different combinations (if you have time), but don't forget to cross out the ones you don't want!*

Finding the maximum and minimum possible values of a calculation (cont.)

Example 2

A toy has a mass of 120g and a volume of 60cm³ (both measurements are correct to the nearest 10 units).

Calculate the lower and upper bounds for the density of the toy.

The upper and lower bounds of the mass are 115g and 125g;
the upper and lower bounds of the volume are 55cm³ and 65cm³.

Lower bound of density = $\frac{115}{65}$ = 1.77g/cm³ (2 d.p.)

Upper bound of density = $\frac{125}{55}$ = 2.27g/cm³ (2 d.p.)

The process for working out the lower and upper bounds in multiplication and addition is quite straightforward. For subtraction and division, more care is needed. Here are a few tips:

- Finding a difference

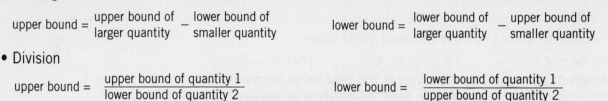

upper bound = $\frac{\text{upper bound of}}{\text{larger quantity}}$ − $\frac{\text{lower bound of}}{\text{smaller quantity}}$ lower bound = $\frac{\text{lower bound of}}{\text{larger quantity}}$ − $\frac{\text{upper bound of}}{\text{smaller quantity}}$

- Division

upper bound = $\frac{\text{upper bound of quantity 1}}{\text{lower bound of quantity 2}}$ lower bound = $\frac{\text{lower bound of quantity 1}}{\text{upper bound of quantity 2}}$

Maximum percentage error

This is found by using the following formula:

Percentage error = $\frac{\text{maximum error}}{\text{original}}$ × 100%

The 'original' is the value that is the furthest from the rounded value.

For the desk in the example on the previous page:

Percentage error = $\frac{5968.75 - 5890}{5890}$ × 100% = 1.34%

Calculations are not always as straightforward as this.

QUICK TEST

1. If $x = \frac{4}{y}$ and $y = 6.2$ (1 d.p.), calculate the upper and lower bounds of x. **C**

2. If $h = ab$, $a = 2.7$ (1 d.p.) and $b = 20$ (to the nearest whole number), calculate the lower and upper bounds of h. **C**

C *Indicates that a calculator may be used.*

Practice questions

Use these questions to test your progress. Check your answers on page 108. You may wish to answer these questions on a separate piece of paper so that you can show full working out

C *Indicates that a calculator may be used.*

1. Mrs Patel inherits £55 000. She divides the money between her children in the ratio 3 : 3 : 5. How much does the child with the largest share receive?

   ....

2. Work these out on your calculator, giving your answers to 3 s.f.
   a) $\dfrac{4.2 \, (3.6 + 5.1)}{2 - 1.9} =$ b) $\dfrac{3.8 + 4.6}{2.9 \times 4.1} =$ **C**

   ....

3. Show how you would estimate the answer to this expression without using a calculator. Work out the estimate.
   $\dfrac{8.7 + 9.02}{0.2 \times 48}$

   ....

   ....

4. Toothpaste is sold in three different-sized tubes.   **C**

   50 ml = £1.24   75 ml = £1.96   100 ml = £2.42
   Which of the tubes of toothpaste is the best value for money?
   You must show full working in order to justify your answer.

   ....

   ....

5. A piece of writing paper is 0.01 cm thick. A notepad has 150 sheets of paper.
   How thick is the notepad?

   ....

6. The price of a CD player has been reduced by 15% in a sale. It now costs £320.   **C**
   What was the original price?

   ....

7. A car was bought in 2004 for £9000. Each year it depreciates in value by 15%.   **C**
   What is the car worth two years later?

   ....

8. James put £632 in a new savings account. At the end of every year, interest at 4.2% is added to his account, based on the amount he had in his savings account at the beginning of that year. Calculate the amount in James's savings account at the end of 3 years.   **C**

   ....

9. The price of a television has risen from £350 to £420.
   Work out the percentage increase in the price.

   ....

10. Write these numbers in standard form:
    a) 2 670 000   b) 4270   c) 0.03296   d) 0.027

    ....

11. The mass of a hair is 0.000042 g.
    a) Write this number in standard form. ....

    b) Calculate, in standard form, the mass of 6×10^5 hairs. ....

12. Work out the answers to these questions giving your answer in standard form:

    a) $(2 \times 10^9) \times (6 \times 10^{12})$ ....

    b) $(8 \times 10^9) \div (4 \times 10^{-2})$ ....

13. y is directly proportional to x. When $x = 4$, $y = 12$. Find: Ⓒ

    a) an equation connecting x and y. ....

    b) the value of x when $y = 20$. ....

14. y is inversely proportional to x^2. When $x = 2$, $y = 5$. Find: Ⓒ

    a) the value of y when $x = 4$. ....

    b) the value of x when $y = 10$. ....

15. Write these recurring decimals as fractions:
    a) $0.\dot{4}$　　　　　b) $0.\dot{2}\dot{1}$　　　　　c) $0.\dot{2}3\dot{4}$　　　　　d) $0.2\dot{7}$

    ....

16. Simplify the following:
    a) $\sqrt{12}$　　　b) $\sqrt{75}$　　　c) $\sqrt{200}$　　　d) $\sqrt{6}(\sqrt{3} - 2)$　　　e) $\sqrt{3} \times \sqrt{75}$

    ....

17. A rectangular carpet is measured as 1.42 m by 1.61 m.
    Find the upper and the lower bounds for the area of the carpet.   Ⓒ

    ....

18. Thomas cycles 1250 m in 95 s. Assuming that the time is measured to the nearest second
    and the distance to the nearest 10 metres, find the upper and lower bounds of
    Thomas' average speed in metres per second.   Ⓒ

    ....

19. The area of a circle is 142 cm² (correct to 3 significant figures).
    Find the upper and lower bounds of the radius of the circle.   Ⓒ

    ....

20. Evaluate the following:

    a) $64^{\frac{1}{3}}$　　b) $8^{\frac{2}{3}}$　　c) 6^{-2}　　d) $49^{\frac{1}{2}}$　　e) $25^{-\frac{1}{2}}$　　f) $(4)^{-2}$　　g) $(\frac{5}{7})^{-2}$

    ....

Algebra 1

In algebra, letters represent numbers.

Algebraic conventions

- A **term** is a collection of numbers, letters and brackets, all multiplied together.
- Terms are separated by + and − signs. Each term has a + or − attached to the front of it.

$$3xy - 5r - 2x^2 + 4$$

invisible + sign xy term r term x^2 term   number term

- An algebraic expression must contain at least one letter.
- $3 \times a$ is written without the multiplication sign as $3a$.

$a + a + a = 3a$

$a \times a \times a = a^3$, **not** $3a$

$a \times a \times 2 = 2a^2$, **not** $(2a)^2$

$a \times b \times 2 = 2ab$

Collecting like terms

Expressions can be simplified by collecting **like terms**.
Only collect the terms if their letters and powers are identical.

Examples
$4a + 2a = 6a$

$3a^2 + 6a^2 - 4a^2 = 5a^2$

$4a + 6b - 3a + 2b = a + 8b$

> Add the a terms together, then the terms with b. Remember a means $1a$.

$9a + 4b$

> Cannot be simplified since there are no like terms.

$3xy + 2yx = 5xy$

> Remember xy means the same as yx.

Writing formulae

Quite often in the exam you are asked to write a formula when given some information or a diagram.

Example
Frances buys x books at £2.50 each. She pays with a £20 note. If she receives C pounds change, write this down as a formula.

> Notice that no £ signs are put in our formula.

$$C = 20 - 2.50x$$

> This is the amount of money she spent.

If in doubt, check by substituting a value for x, e.g.:
if she bought 1 book $x = 1$, so her change would be
$20 - 2.50 \times 1 = £17.50$ ✔

Example
Some patterns are made by using grey and white paving slabs.

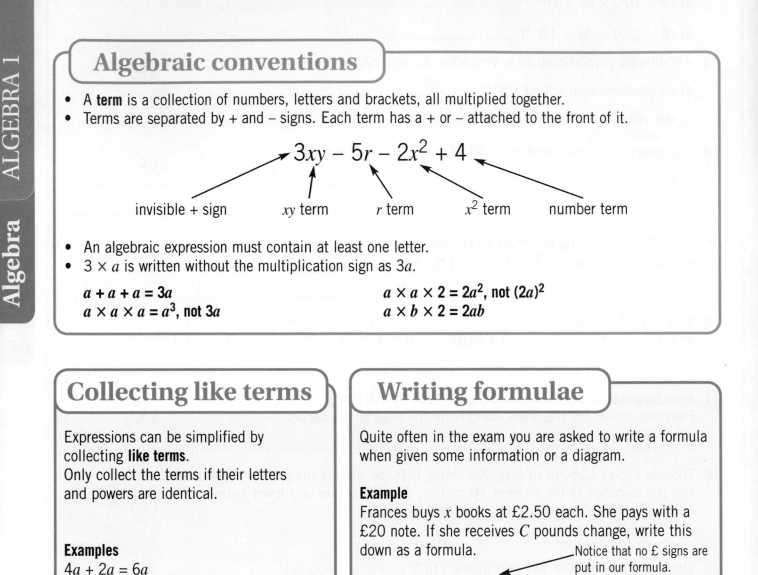

Write a formula for the number of grey paving slabs (g) in a pattern that uses w white ones.
Formula is $g = 2w + 2$

$2w$ represents the 2 layers, + 2 gives the grey slabs on either end of the white ones.

Formulae, expressions and substituting

$p + 3$ is an **expression**.

$y = p + 3$ is a **formula**. The value of y depends on the value of p.

Replacing a letter with a number is called **substitution**. When substituting:

- Write out the expressions first and then replace the letters with the values given.
- Work out the value on your calculator. Use bracket keys where possible and pay attention to the order of operations.

Examples

Using $W = 5.6$, $t = -7.1$ and $u = 2$, find the value of these expressions, giving your answers to 3 s.f.

a) $\frac{W+t}{u}$ b) $W - \frac{t}{u}$ c) $\sqrt{Wt^2}$

You may need to treat t^2 as $(-7.1)^2$, depending on your calculator.

Remember to show the substitutions.

a) $\frac{W+t}{u} = \frac{5.6 + (-7.1)}{2} = -0.75$

b) $W - \frac{t}{u} = 5.6 - \frac{(-7.1)}{2} = 9.15$

c) $\sqrt{Wt^2} = \sqrt{5.6 \times (-7.1)^2} = 16.8$

> **When substituting into an expression or formula you must show each step of your working out. By showing your substitutions, you will obtain method marks even if you get the final answer wrong.**

Using formulae

A formula describes the relationship between two (or more) variables.

A formula must have an equals sign (=) in it.

Example

Andrew hires a van. There is a standing charge of £8 and then it costs £3 per hour.

How much does it cost for:
a) 6 hours' drive   b) y hours' drive
c) Write a formula for the total hire cost C.

a) $8 + (3 \times 6) = £26$
b) $8 + (3 \times y) = £(8 + 3y)$
c) $C = 8 + 3y$

This is a formula which works out the cost of hiring the van for any number of hours.

KEY TERMS

Make sure you understand these terms before moving on!

- term
- expression
- formula
- substitution

QUICK TEST

1. Simplify these expressions by collecting like terms.
   a) $5a + 2a + 3a$
   b) $6a - 3b + 4b + 2a$
   c) $5x - 3x + 7x - 2y + 6y$
   d) $3xy^2 - 2x^2y + 6x^2y - 8xy^2$

2. Using $p = 6.2$, $r = -3.2$ and $s = 3$, find the value of these expressions, giving your answers to 3 s.f. Use a calculator.
   a) $pr + s$ b) $p^2s - r$
   c) $r^2 - \frac{p}{s}$ d) $(ps - r)^2$

C

Algebra 2

Multiplying out brackets

- Multiplying out brackets helps to simplify algebraic expressions.
- The term outside the brackets multiplies each separate term inside the brackets.

Examples

$3(2x + 5) = 6x + 15$ $(3 \times 2x = 6x, 3 \times 5 = 15)$

$a(3a - 4) = 3a^2 - 4a$ $b(2a + 3b - c) = 2ab + 3b^2 - bc$

- If the term outside the bracket is negative, all of the signs of the terms inside the bracket are changed when multiplying out.

Examples

$-4(2x + 3) = -8x - 12$

$-2(4 - 3x) = -8 + 6x$

> If you are asked to expand brackets it just means multiply them out. When you have finished multiplying out the brackets, simplify by collecting like terms in order to pick up the final mark.

To simplify expressions, first expand the brackets then collect like terms.

Examples

Expand and simplify $2(x - 3) + x(x + 4)$.
$2(x - 3) + x(x + 4)$
$= 2x - 6 + x^2 + 4x$ Multiply out the brackets.
$= x^2 + 6x - 6$ Collect like terms.

Expand and simplify $6y - 2(y - 3)$
$6y - 2(y - 3)$
$= 6y - 2y + 6$ Take care with multiplying by
$= 4y + 6$ a negative number.

Multiplication of two brackets

Each term in the first bracket is multiplied by each term in the second; simplify by collecting like terms.

Examples
Expand and simplify the following.

a) $(x + 2)(x + 3) = x(x + 3) + 2(x + 3)$
$= x^2 + 3x + 2x + 6$
$= x^2 + 5x + 6$

b) $(2x + 4)(3x - 2) = 2x(3x - 2) + 4(3x - 2)$
$= 6x^2 - 4x + 12x - 8$
$= 6x^2 + 8x - 8$

c) $(x + y)^2 \equiv x(x + y) + y(x + y)$
$\equiv x^2 + xy + xy + y^2$
$\equiv x^2 + 2xy + y^2$ (this is an identity; it is true for all values of x.)

> A common error is to think that $(a + b)^2$ means $a^2 + b^2$.

Rearranging formulae

The **subject of a formula** is the letter that appears on its own on one side of the formula.

Examples
Make p the subject of these formulae:

a) $r = (p + 6)^2$ b) $y = \dfrac{p + r}{6}$

a) $r = (p + 6)^2$ Deal with the power first. Take the square root of both sides.

$\sqrt{r} = p + 6$ Remove any terms added or subtracted. So subtract 6 from both sides.

$\sqrt{r} - 6 = p$ **or** $p = \sqrt{r} - 6$
The subject of the formula is usually written first.

b) $y = \dfrac{p + r}{6}$ First deal with the term dividing p; multiply both sides by 6.

$6y = p + r$ Remove r by subtracting r from both sides.

$6y - r = p$ **or** $p = 6y - r$

Factorisation (putting brackets in)

Factorisation is the reverse of expanding brackets. An expression is put into brackets by taking out **common factors**.

Example

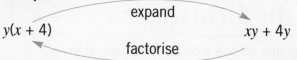

$y(x + 4)$ expand $xy + 4y$

factorise

To **factorise** $xy + 4y$:
- Recognise that y is a factor of each term.
- Take out the common factor.
- The expression is completed inside the bracket, so that the result is equivalent to $xy + 4y$ when multiplied out.

Examples

Factorise the following:

a) $5x^2 + x = x(5x + 1)$

b) $4x^2 + 8x = 4x(x + 2)$

c) $5x^3 + 15x^4 = 5x^3(1 + 3x)$

Factorising can be useful when simplifying algebraic fractions.

Example

Simplify $\dfrac{5x + 15}{x + 3}$.

$\dfrac{5x + 15}{x + 3} = \dfrac{5(x + 3)}{(x + 3)} = 5$

Factorisation of a quadratic

Two brackets are obtained when a quadratic expression of the type $x^2 + bx + c$ is factorised.

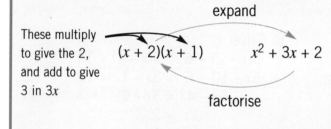

These multiply to give the 2, and add to give 3 in $3x$ $(x + 2)(x + 1)$ expand $x^2 + 3x + 2$ factorise

Examples

Factorise the following expressions:
a) $x^2 + 5x - 6 = (x - 1)(x + 6)$
b) $x^2 - 6x + 8 = (x - 2)(x - 4)$
c) $x^2 - 25 = (x - 5)(x + 5)$

Example c) is known as the 'difference of two squares'.
In general, $x^2 - a^2 = (x - a)(x + a)$.

QUICK TEST

1. Multiply out the brackets and simplify where possible.
   a) $3(x + 2)$ b) $2(x + y)$
   c) $-3(2x + 4)$ d) $(x + 2)(x + 3)$
   e) $(y - 4)(y - 3)$ f) $(a + 2)^2$

2. Factorise the following expressions:
   a) $3x + 9$ b) $5y - 15$
   c) $12x^2 - 6x$ d) $x^2 - 5x - 6$
   e) $x^2 - 3x + 2$ f) $x^2 - 16$

3. Make u the subject of the formula $v^2 = u^2 + 2as$.

4. $V = IR$. Make R the subject of the formula.

Equations 1

An equation involves an unknown value which has to be worked out.

Solving linear equations of the form $ax + b = cx + d$

The trick with **linear equations** is to get all the x-terms together on one side of the equals sign and the numbers on the other side.

Example

Solve
$$5x - 9 = 12 - 4x$$
$$9x - 9 = 12 \qquad \text{Add } 4x \text{ to both sides.}$$
$$9x = 21 \qquad \text{Add 9 to both sides.}$$
$$x = \tfrac{21}{9} = 2\tfrac{1}{3}$$

If in the exam you do not know that $\tfrac{21}{9} = 2\tfrac{1}{3}$, leave it as $\tfrac{21}{9}$ to obtain full marks!

Solving linear equations with brackets

Just because an equation has brackets, don't be put off. The method is just the same as for the other equations once the brackets have been multiplied out.

Examples

a) Solve:
$$3(x - 2) = 2(x + 6)$$
$$3x - 6 = 2x + 12 \qquad \text{Multiply out the brackets first.}$$
$$x - 6 = 12$$
$$x = 18$$

b) Solve:
$$5(x - 2) + 6 = 3(x - 4) + 10$$
$$5x - 10 + 6 = 3x - 12 + 10$$
$$5x - 4 = 3x - 2$$
$$2x = 2$$
$$x = 1$$

Solving quadratic equations

Make sure the **quadratic equation** is equal to zero. Then factorise the quadratic equation.

Examples

Solve the following equations.

a) $x^2 - 5x = 0$ **x is a common factor.**
$x(x - 5) = 0$
Either $x = 0$ or $x - 5 = 0$, i.e. $x = 5$.

b) $x^2 - 3x = 10$
$x^2 - 3x - 10 = 0$ Make it equal to zero, then factorise.
$(x + 2)(x - 5) = 0$
Either $(x + 2) = 0$, i.e. $x = -2$, or $(x - 5) = 0$, i.e. $x = 5$.

Solving equations involving indices

Equations sometimes involve indices. You will need to remember the laws of indices to be able to solve them. (Look back at pages 22–23 if you aren't sure of them.)

Examples

1. **Solve**

$$y^k = \sqrt{y} \div \frac{1}{y^4}$$
$$y^k = y^{\frac{1}{2}} \div y^{-4}$$
$$y^k = y^{\frac{1}{2} -(-4)}$$
$$y^k = y^{4\frac{1}{2}} \quad \text{Compare indices}$$
$$k = 4\frac{1}{2}$$

2. Solve

$$4^{k+1} = 16$$
$$4^{k+1} = 4^2 \quad \text{Rewrite so that the bases}$$
$$k + 1 = 2 \quad \text{are the same.}$$
$$k = 1$$

Using equations to solve problems

Example

The perimeter of the triangle is 20 cm.
Work out the value of x and hence find
the length of the 3 sides.

$$x + (2x + 5) + (4x + 1) = 20 \quad \text{The perimeter is found by adding lengths together.}$$

Collect like terms and solve the equation as before.

$$7x + 6 = 20$$
$$7x = 20 - 6$$
$$7x = 14$$
$$x = \frac{14}{7} = 2$$

So the lengths of the sides are
2 (= x), 9 (= 2x + 5) and 9 (= 4x + 1).
9 (= 4x + 1)
9(2x + 5)

*Solving equations is a very common topic at GCSE.
Try to work through them in a logical way, always
showing full working out. If you have time, check your
answer by substituting it back into the equation to see
if it works.*

KEY TERMS

Make sure you
understand these
terms before moving on!

- linear equation
- quadratic equation
- solve

QUICK TEST

Solve the following equations:

1. $2x - 3 = 9$
2. $4x + 2 = 20$
3. $5x + 3 = 2x + 9$
4. $6x - 1 = 15 + 2x$
5. $3(x + 2) = x + 4$
6. $2(x - 1) = 6(2x + 2)$
7. $x^2 + 4x - 5 = 0$
8. $x^2 - 5x + 6 = 0$
9. $4^{2k-1} = 32$

Equations 2

Simultaneous equations

Two equations with two unknowns are called **simultaneous equations**.
They can be solved in several ways. Solving equations simultaneously involves finding values for the letters that will make both equations work.

Graphical method

The points at which any two graphs intersect represent the simultaneous solutions of these equations.

Example

Solve the simultaneous equations $y = 2x - 1$ and $x + y = 5$.
- Draw the two graphs.

$$y = 2x - 1 \qquad \text{If } x = 0, y = -1.$$
$$\text{If } y = 0, x = \tfrac{1}{2}.$$

$$x + y = 5 \qquad \text{If } x = 0, y = 5.$$
$$\text{If } x = 5, y = 0.$$

- At the point of intersection $x = 2$ and $y = 3$.

Point of intersection (2, 3)

Elimination method

If the **coefficient** of one of the letters is the same in both equations, then that letter may be eliminated by subtracting the equations.

Example

Solve simultaneously $2x + 3y = 6$ and $x + y = 1$.

Step 1

Label the equations ① and ②.

$$2x + 3y = 6 \qquad ①$$
$$x + y = 1 \qquad ②$$

$\times 2$

> Simultaneous equations can be difficult to master. Try to learn the steps outlined here and practise lots of examples. Use the check at the end to make sure that you have the correct answers.

Step 2

Since no coefficients match, multiply equation ② by 2. Rename it equation ③.

$$2x + 3y = 6 \qquad ①$$
$$2x + 2y = 2 \qquad ③$$

The coefficient is the number a letter is multiplied by, e.g. the coefficient of $-2x$ is -2.

Step 3

The coefficient of x in equations ① and ③ are the same. Subtract equation ③ from equation ① and then solve the remaining equation.

$$0x + y = 4$$
$$\therefore y = 4$$

> **Remember:**
> - to eliminate terms with opposite signs, add the equations
> - to eliminate terms with the same signs, subtract the equations.

Step 4

Substitute the value $y = 4$ into equation ① or equation ②. Solve the resulting equation to find x.

$$x + 4 = 1$$
$$x = 1 - 4$$
$$x = -3$$

Step 5

Check in equation ①.

The solution is $x = -3$, $y = 4$.

$$(2 \times -3) + (3 \times 4) = 6$$
$$-6 + 12 = 6 \ \checkmark$$

Solving cubic equations by trial and improvement

Trial and improvement gives an approximate solution to **cubic equations**.

Example
The equation $x^3 - 5x = 10$ has a solution between 2 and 3. Find this solution to 2 decimal places.

Draw a table to help.
Substitute different values of x into $x^3 - 5x$.

x	$x^3 - 5x$	Comment
2.5	3.125	too small
2.8	7.952	too small
2.9	9.889	too small
2.95	10.922375	too big
2.94	10.712184	too big
2.91	10.092171	too big

At this stage the solution is trapped between 2.90 and 2.91. Checking the middle value, $x = 2.905$, gives $x^3 - 5x = 9.99036 \ldots$ which is too small.

```
  2.90              2.905              2.91
(too small)      (too small)        (too big)
```

The diagram makes it clear that the solution correct to 2 decimal places is 2.91.

💡 *Make sure you write down the solution of x, not the answer to $x^3 - 5x$.*

QUICK TEST

❶ Solve the following pairs of simultaneous equations:

a) $4x + 7y = 10$
   $2x + 3y = 3$

b) $3a - 5b = 1$
   $2a + 3b = 7$

❷ The diagram shows the graphs of the equations $x + y = 2$ and $y = x - 4$.
Use the diagram to solve the simultaneous equations
$x + y = 2$
$y = x - 4$

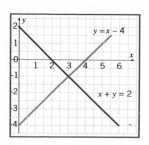

❸ The equation $y^3 + y = 40$ has a solution between 3 and 4. Find this solution to 1 d.p. by using a method of trial and improvement.

Further algebra & equations

Quadratic equations

We have already seen how to factorise a quadratic equation of the form $x^2 + bx + c = 0$ (page 35). Unfortunately, they are not all as easy as this, and so there are several other methods for solving quadratic equations of the form $ax^2 + bx + c = 0$.

Factorisation

Example: Solve $3x^2 - x - 4 = 0$.
a) Write out the two brackets and put an x in one and $3x$ in the other, since $x \times 3x = 3x^2$.
b) We now need two numbers that multiply to give –4 (one positive and one negative) and, when multiplied by the x terms, add up to $-1x$.
   $(3x - 4)(x + 1) = 3x^2 - x - 4$
c) Now solve the equation $(3x - 4)(x + 1) = 0$.
   Put each bracket equal to 0.
   $(3x - 4) = 0$ so $x = \frac{4}{3}$ **or** $(x + 1) = 0$ so $x = -1$

The quadratic formula

This formula can be used to solve any quadratic equation. Only use this equation, though, if the quadratic equation cannot be factorised.

$$x = \frac{-b \ \pm\sqrt{b^2 - 4ac}}{2a} \quad \text{for any quadratic equation written in the form } ax^2 + bx + c = 0.$$

Example: Find the solutions of $2x^2 + x = 7$ to 2 decimal places.
a) Put the equation into the form $ax^2 + bx + c = 0$: $2x^2 + x - 7 = 0$
b) Identify the values of a, b and c: $a = 2$, $b = 1$, $c = -7$
c) Substitute these values into the quadratic formula:

$$x = \frac{-b \ \pm\sqrt{b^2 - 4ac}}{2a} \qquad x = \frac{-1 \pm \sqrt{1^2 - (4 \times 2 \times -7)}}{2 \times 2} = \frac{-1 \pm\sqrt{1 + 56}}{4} = \frac{-1 \pm\sqrt{57}}{4}$$

One solution is when we use $-\sqrt{57}$:   The other solution is when we use $+\sqrt{57}$:

$$x = \frac{-1 - \sqrt{57}}{4} = -2.14 \qquad\qquad x = \frac{-1 + \sqrt{57}}{4} = 1.64$$

d) To check, put these values into the original equation.
   $2 \times (-2.14)^2 + (-2.14) = 7$ ✓ $2 \times (1.64)^2 + (1.64) = 7$ ✓

Completing the square

This is the method used when quadratic equations are expressed in the form $(x + a)^2 + b = 0$.
- Rearrange the equation in the form $ax^2 + bx + c = 0$. If a is not 1, then divide the whole equation by a.
- Write the equation in the form $(x + \frac{b}{2})^2$. Notice that the number in the bracket is always half the value of b!
- Multiply out the brackets, compare to the original and adjust by adding or subtracting an extra amount.

Example: Express $x^2 - 4x + 1 = 0$ as a completed square and, hence, solve it.

1) $x^2 - 4x + 1 = 0$ This is already in the form $ax^2 + bx + c = 0$ and $a = 1$.
2) $(x - 2)^2$ Half of –4 is –2.
3) $(x - 2)^2 = x^2 - 4x + 4$ Multiply out the brackets and now compare to the original $x^2 - 4x + 1$.
                      To make $x^2 - 4x + 4$ like the original we need to subtract 3.
4) So $(x - 2)^2 - 3 = 0$ Now we need to solve the equation.
       $(x - 2)^2 = 3$
       $(x - 2) = \pm \sqrt{3}$ $\therefore x = \sqrt{3} + 2$ or $x = -\sqrt{3} + 2$
                        $x = 3.73$ $x = 0.27$

Algebraic fractions

When working with algebraic fractions, the rules are the same as for ordinary fractions.

a) Addition and subtraction
Always find a common denominator (the same bottom line) and then adjust the numerators. Simplify by multiplying out the numerator and collecting like terms.

Example

$$\frac{x+2}{x-1} + \frac{3}{x} = \frac{x(x+2)}{x(x-1)} + \frac{3(x-1)}{x(x-1)} =$$

$$\frac{x^2 + 2x + 3x - 3}{x(x-1)} = \frac{x^2 + 5x - 3}{x(x-1)}$$

b) Multiplication
Simply multiply the numerators together and the denominators together and cancel if possible.

Example

$$\frac{3p^2q}{r^2s} \times \frac{2rs}{9pq^2} = \frac{2p}{3qr}$$

c) Division
Remember to turn the second fraction upside down (i.e. take the reciprocal), then multiply and cancel if possible.

Example

$$\frac{6(x+2)}{(x-1)} \div \frac{12(x+2)(x+3)}{(x+1)}$$

$$= \frac{\cancel{6(x+2)}}{(x-1)} \times \frac{(x+1)}{\cancel{12(x+2)}(x+3)}$$

$$= \frac{(x+1)}{2(x-1)(x+3)}$$

Rearranging formulae when the subject appears in more than one term

Example
Make y the subject of the formula $\quad a = \dfrac{y+b}{y-c}$

$$a = \frac{y+b}{y-c}$$

$a(y-c) = y+b$	Multiply both sides by $(y-c)$.
$ay - ac = y + b$	Multiply out the brackets.
$ay - y = b + ac$	Collect the terms involving y on one side of the equation.
$y(a-1) = b + ac$	Factorise.

So $\quad y = \dfrac{b+ac}{a-1}$

> 🛈 **All the techniques outlined in this section are very important! Practise plenty of questions on these topics to help you become confident when working with more complex algebra. GCSE questions on these topics usually carry a lot of marks.**

QUICK TEST

1. Solve the following quadratic equations by a) factorisation, b) quadratic formula and c) completing the square.

   a) $3x^2 - 7x + 2 = 0$ b) $2x^2 + 5x + 2 = 0$ c) $4x^2 - 7x - 2 = 0$

2. Make r the subject of the formula $\quad p = \dfrac{r-y}{r+s}$.

3. Simplify the following algebraic fractions:

   a) $\dfrac{2}{(x+2)} + \dfrac{3}{(x-1)}$ b) $\dfrac{4(s-1)}{3(s+2)} \times \dfrac{(s+2)^2}{8(s-3)}$

   c) $\dfrac{8(a^2-b^2)}{3(a+2)} \quad \dfrac{4(a-b)}{27(a+1)}$

Inequalities

Inequalities are solved in a similar way to equations.

The four inequality symbols

> means 'greater than'
< means 'less than'
So $x > 3$ and $3 < x$ both say 'x is greater than 3'.

$\geqslant$ means 'greater than or equal to'
$\leqslant$ means 'less than or equal to'

- Dividing by a negative number reverses the direction of the inequality sign:

$$-2x < 6$$
$$x > \frac{6}{-2}$$
$$x > -3$$

Examples
Solve the following inequalities:

a)
$4x - 2$	$< 2x + 6$	
$2x - 2$	< 6	Subtract $2x$ from both sides.
$2x$	< 8	Add 2 to both sides.
x	< 4	Divide both sides by 2.

The solution of this inequality can be represented on a number line:

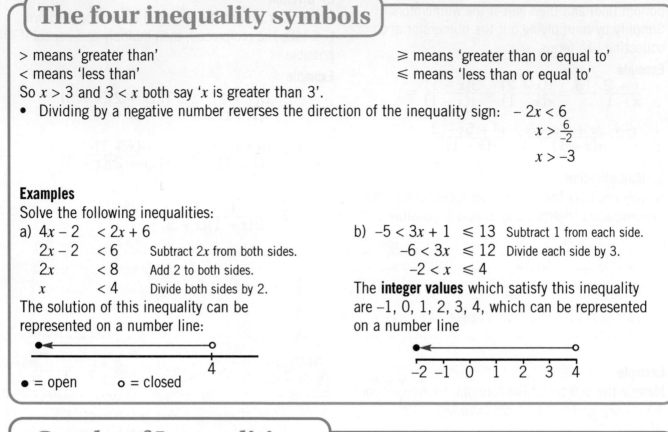

● = open   o = closed

b)
$-5 < 3x + 1$	$\leqslant 13$	Subtract 1 from each side.
$-6 < 3x$	$\leqslant 12$	Divide each side by 3.
$-2 < x$	$\leqslant 4$	

The **integer values** which satisfy this inequality are -1, 0, 1, 2, 3, 4, which can be represented on a number line

Graphs of Inequalities

The graph of an equation such as $y = 3$ is a line, whereas the graph of the inequality $y < 3$ is a region which has the line $y = 3$ as its **boundary**.

To show the region for given inequalities:

- Draw the boundary lines first.

- For **strict** inequalities > and <, the boundary line is not included and is shown as a dotted line.

- It is often easier with several inequalities to shade out the unwanted regions, so that the solution is shown **unshaded** (as in the example).

Example

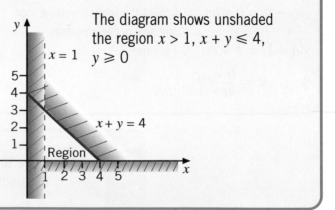

The diagram shows unshaded the region $x > 1$, $x + y \leqslant 4$, $y \geqslant 0$

Solve the following inequalities:

1. $2x - 3 < 9$

2. $5x + 1 \geqslant 21$

3. $1 \leqslant 3x - 2 \leqslant 7$

4. $1 \leqslant 5x + 2 < 12$

Make sure you understand these terms before moving on!
KEY TERMS
- inequality
- region

Number patterns & sequences

Sequences

A **sequence** is a list of numbers. There is usually a relationship between the numbers.
Each number in the list is called a **term**.

Example
The odd numbers form a sequence 1, 3, 5, 7, 9, 11, ..., in which the terms have a **common difference** of 2.

1 ⌣ 3 ⌣ 5 ⌣ 7 ⌣ 9 ⌣ 11 ...
  2   2   2   2   2

Important number sequences

Square numbers: 1, 4, 9, 16, 25, ...	Triangular numbers: 1, 3, 6, 10, 15, ...
Cube numbers: 1, 8, 27, 64, 125, ...	The Fibonacci sequence: 1, 1, 2, 3, 5, 8, 13, ...
Powers of 2: 1, 2, 4, 8, 16, ...	Powers of 10: 1, 10, 100, 1000, ...

Finding the nth term of a linear sequence

The nth term gives an expression for the term in the nth position.

The nth term of a sequence is more efficient as it allows any term in a sequence to be found without relying on knowing the previous term.

The nth term of a linear sequence is of the form **$an+b$**.

Example
Find an expression for the nth term of this sequence: 3, 5, 7, 9,...

Find the common difference; this is a.
Difference = 2, so $a = 2$
So the nth term = $2n + b$

Term	1	2	3	4	.... n
Number in sequence	3	5	7	9	....

- Now substitute the value of $n = 1$ and the number in the sequence, in this case it is 3.

nth term = $2n + b$
$3 = 2 \times 1 + b$
$3 = 2 + b$
$3 - 2 = b$
$b = 1$, so $b = 1$

nth term is $2n + 1$
- **check when $n = 2$** $2 \times 2 + 1 = 5$ number in sequence is 5 so the nth term is $2n + 1$

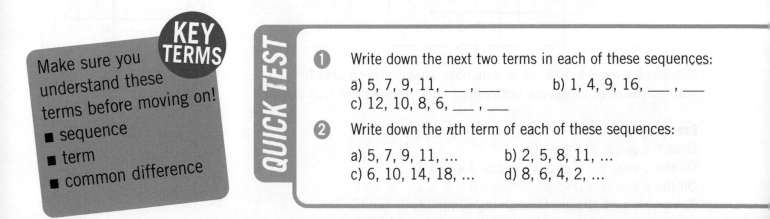

KEY TERMS

Make sure you understand these terms before moving on!
- sequence
- term
- common difference

QUICK TEST

① Write down the next two terms in each of these sequences:
a) 5, 7, 9, 11, ___ , ___   b) 1, 4, 9, 16, ___ , ___
c) 12, 10, 8, 6, ___ , ___

② Write down the nth term of each of these sequences:
a) 5, 7, 9, 11, ...   b) 2, 5, 8, 11, ...
c) 6, 10, 14, 18, ...   d) 8, 6, 4, 2, ...

Straight line graphs

Drawing straight line graphs

In order to draw a straight line graph, follow these easy steps:

Step 1
Choose 3 values of x and draw up a table.

Step 2
Work out the value of y for each value of x.

Step 3
Plot the coordinates and join up the points with a straight line.

Step 4
Label the graph.

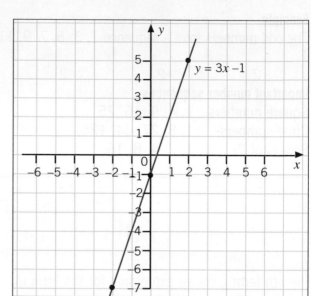

Example
Draw the graph of $y = 3x - 1$.

Draw up a table with some suitable values of x.
Work out the y values by putting each x value into the equation.
e.g. $x = -2$ ∴ $y = (3 \times -2) - 1$
$= -6 - 1 = -7$

x	−2	0	2
y	−7	−1	5

Plot the points and draw the line.

> 💡 **You need to be able to sketch a straight line graph from its equation. If you can do this then you will be able to tell if the graph you have drawn is correct.**

Graphs of $y = a$, $x = b$ and $x + y = k$

$y = a$ is a horizontal line with every y coordinate equal to a.

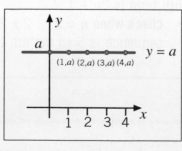

$x = b$ is a vertical line with every x coordinate equal to b.

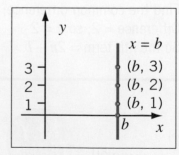

Graphs of $x + y = k$, where k is a number, always give straight line graphs. Tables of values are not needed when drawing this type of graph.

Example
Draw the graph of $x + y = 3$
On the x axis, $y = 0$ so $x = 3$ since $3 + 0 = 3$
On the y axis, $x = 0$ so $y = 3$ since $0 + 3 = 3$
The graph goes straight through the points (3, 0) and (0, 3).

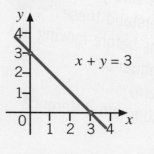

Interpreting $y = mx + c$

The general equation of a straight line graph is
$$y = mx + c$$

where m is the gradient (steepness) of the line.

- As m increases the line gets steeper.
- If m is positive, the line slopes forwards.
- If m is negative, the line slopes backwards.

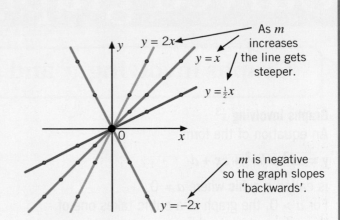

As m increases the line gets steeper.

m is negative so the graph slopes 'backwards'.

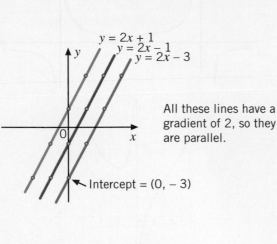

All these lines have a gradient of 2, so they are parallel.

Intercept = (0, − 3)

- c is the **intercept** on the y axis, that is, where the graph cuts the y axis.

- **Parallel** lines have the same gradient.

- If two lines are **perpendicular** the product of their gradients is –1.
  If a line has a gradient of m, then a line which is perpendicular to it will have a gradient of $\frac{-1}{m}$.
  In the diagram above, the lines $y = -2x$ and $y = \frac{1}{2}x$ are perpendicular because $-2 \times \frac{1}{2} = -1$.

Finding the gradient of a line

- To find the **gradient** (steepness) of a line, choose two points.
- Draw a triangle as shown.
- Find the change in y (height) and the change in x (base).

- gradient $= \dfrac{\text{change in } y}{\text{change in } x}$ or $\dfrac{\text{height}}{\text{base}} = \dfrac{4}{3} = 1\frac{1}{3}$

- Decide if the gradient is positive or negative.

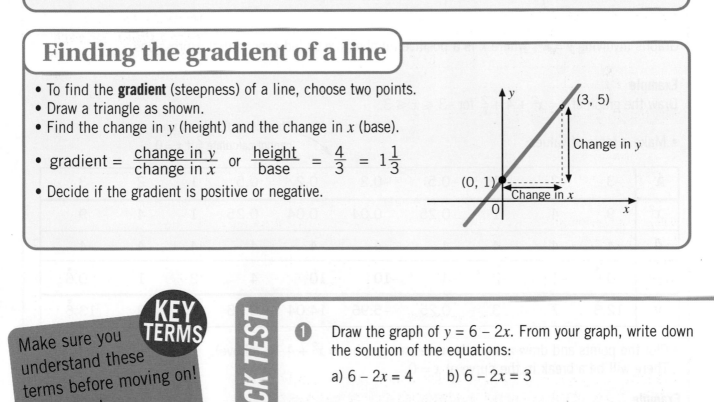

(3, 5)

Change in y

(0, 1)

Change in x

QUICK TEST

1. Draw the graph of $y = 6 - 2x$. From your graph, write down the solution of the equations:

   a) $6 - 2x = 4$ b) $6 - 2x = 3$

2. Write down the gradient and y axis intercept for each of these straight line graphs:

   a) $y = 4 + 2x$ b) $y = 3x - 2$ c) $2y = 6x + 4$

Curved graphs

Graphs involving x^3 and $\frac{1}{x}$

Graphs involving x^3

An equation of the form

$$y = ax^3 + bx^2 + cx + d$$

is called a **cubic** where $a \neq 0$.
For $a > 0$, the graph of a cubic takes one of these forms:

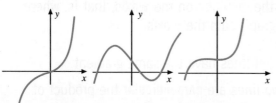

For $a < 0$, the overall trend is reversed:

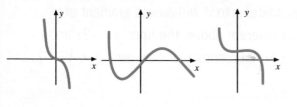

Graphs involving $\frac{1}{x}$

An equation of the form $y = \frac{a}{x}$ takes two basic forms depending on the value of a.

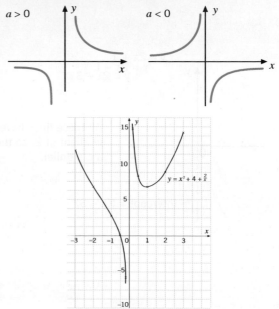

Graphs involving $y = k^x$, where k is a positive number, are called exponential expressions.

Example
Draw the graph of $y = x^2 + 4 + \frac{2}{x}$ for $-3 \leqslant x \leqslant 3$.

• Make a table of values:

There is no 0 column since you cannot calculate $\frac{2}{x}$ if $x = 0$.

x	-3	-2	-1	-0.5	-0.2	0.2	0.5	1	2	3
x^2	9	4	1	0.25	0.04	0.04	0.25	1	4	9
4	4	4	4	4	4	4	4	4	4	4
$+\frac{2}{x}$	$-0.\dot{6}$	-1	-2	-4	-10	10	4	2	1	$0.\dot{6}$
y	$12.\dot{3}$	7	3	0.25	-5.96	14.04	8.25	7	9	$13.\dot{6}$

• Plot the points and draw a smooth curve (see graph $y = x^2 + 4 + \frac{2}{x}$ above).
  There will be a break in the curve at $x = 0$.

Example
A sketch of the graph $y = 2^x$ looks like the graph opposite:

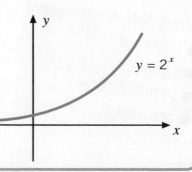

The graph $y = 2^x$ has no maximum or minimum point. It crosses the y axis at the point (0, 1). The value of y increases rapidly as the value of x increases. When x is negative the value of y approaches zero. The graph never crosses the x axis.

Graphs of the form $y = ax^2 + bx + c$

These are called **quadratic graphs** where $a \neq 0$.
These graphs are curved and known as **parabolas**.
If $a > 0$, then the graph is U-shaped.
If $a < 0$, then the graph has an upside-down U.

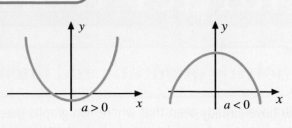

Example
Draw the graph of $y = x^2 - x - 6$ using values of x from –2 to 3.
Use the graph to find the value of x when $y = -3$.

• Make a table of values. Work out the values of y by substituting the values of x into the equation:
  e.g. If $x = 1$ $y = x^2 - x - 6 = 1^2 - 1 - 6 = -6$

x	–2	–1	0	1	2	3	0.5
y	0	–4	–6	–6	–4	0	–6.25

$x = 0.5$ is worked out to find the minimum value.

• Plot the points and join them with a smooth curve.
• The **minimum value** is when $x = 0.5$, $y = -6.25$.
• The **line of symmetry** is at $x = 0.5$.
• The curve cuts the y axis at (0, –6), i.e. (0, c).
• When $y = -3$, read across from $y = -3$ to the graph then read up to the x axis: $x = 2.3$ and $x = -1.3$.
  These are the approximate solutions of the equation $x^2 - x - 6 = -3$.

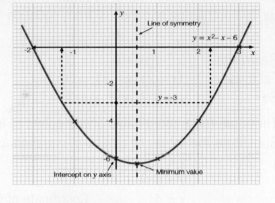

💡 *Draw the curve with a sharp pencil, go through all the points and check for any parts that look wrong.*

QUICK TEST

❶ a) Complete the table of values for the graph $y = x^3 + 3$.

x	–3	–2	–1	0	1	2	3
y							

b) Draw the graph of $y = x^3 + 3$. Use scales of 1 unit per 2 cm on the x axis and 10 units per 2 cm on the y axis.
c) From your graph, find the value of x when $y = 15$.

❷ Match each of the four graphs below with one of the following equations:
a) $y = 2x - 5$ b) $y = x^2 + 3$ c) $y = 3 - x^2$
d) $y = 5 - x$ e) $y = x^3$ f) $y = \frac{2}{x}$

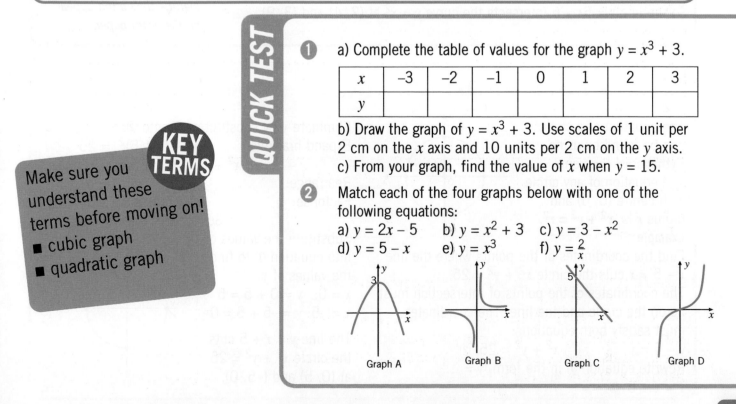

Graph A   Graph B   Graph C   Graph D

Harder work on graphs

Solving quadratic and linear equations simultaneously

We have already seen that where two graphs meet, this represents the simultaneous solutions of the equations. So far we have only looked at linear equations and their corresponding straight line graphs. You also need to be able to work out the coordinates of the points of intersection of a straight line and a quadratic curve.

The diagram shows the points of intersection of the straight line $y = 5x - 6$ and the curve $y = x^2$.

To find the coordinates of the points of intersection, C and D, of the line $y = 5x - 6$ and the curve $y = x^2$, we know that the points C and D both lie on the curve and the line, giving us the simultaneous equations

$y = 5x - 6$ ① $y = x^2$ ②

Eliminate y by substituting equation ② into equation ① (or by subtracting equation ① from equation ②):

$$x^2 = 5x - 6$$

Rearrange: $x^2 - 5x + 6 = 0$

Factorise: $(x - 2)(x - 3) = 0$

So $x = 2$ and $x = 3$

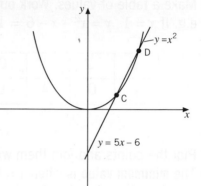

These are the x coordinates of the points of intersection.
Substitute the values of x back in equation ① to find the y coordinates:

$x = 2$:
$y = 5x - 6$
$y = 5 \times 2 - 6$
$y = 4$ Coordinate of C (2, 4)

$x = 3$:
$y = 5x - 6)$
$y = 5 \times 3 - 6$
$y = 9$ Coordinate of D (3, 9)

So the line $y = 5x - 6$ intersects the curve $y = x^2$ at (2, 4) and (3, 9).

> **Remember, solving a quadratic and a linear equation gives the point of intersection of the two graphs. There are some quite difficult topics in this section. The four graph transformations need to be learnt – they often appear on the exam paper.**

The intersection of a circle and a line

The equation of a circle can be found by using Pythagoras' theorem.
The equation of any circle with centre (0, 0) and radius r is $x^2 + y^2 = r^2$.

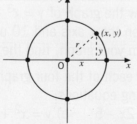

Example
Find the coordinates of the points where the line $y - 5 = x$ cuts the circle $x^2 + y^2 = 25$.
The coordinates of the points of intersection must lie on the circle and the line. The coordinates must satisfy both equations:

$y - 5 = x$ ① $x^2 + y^2 = 25$ ②

Rewrite equation ① in the form '$y = ...$'

$y = x + 5$ ①

Eliminate y by substituting ① into ②.
Expand brackets: $x^2 + (x + 5)^2 = 25$
$x^2 + x^2 + 10x + 25 = 25$
Rearrange: $2x^2 + 10x = 0$
Factorise: $2x(x + 5) = 0$
So $x = 0$ or $x = -5$.

Substitute the values of x into equation ① to find the values of y:

$x = 0$: $y = 0 + 5 = 5$
$x = -5$: $y = -5 + 5 = 0$

The line $y = x + 5$ cuts the circle $x^2 + y^2 = 25$ at (0, 5) and (-5, 0).

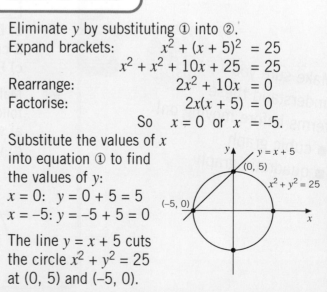

Functions and transformations

If $y =$ 'an expression involving x' then it can be written as $y = f(x)$.
The graphs of related functions can be found by applying the following **transformations**.

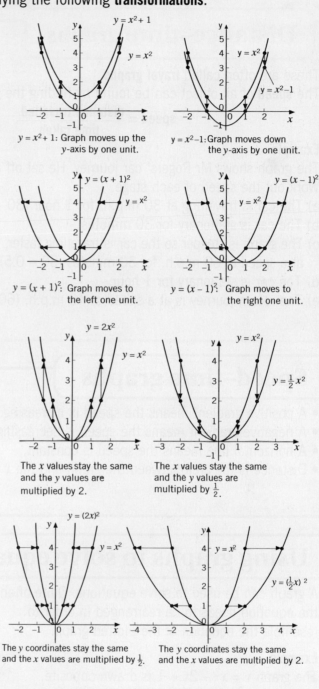

- $y = f(x) \pm a$ moves the graphs up or down the y-axis by a value of a.

  $y = x^2 + 1$: Graph moves up the y-axis by one unit.

  $y = x^2 - 1$: Graph moves down the y-axis by one unit.

- $y = f(x \pm a)$ moves the whole graph a units to the left or right. They move in the opposite direction to what you would think!
  $y = f(x + a)$ moves the graph a units to the left.
  $y = f(x - a)$ moves the graph a units to the right.

  $y = (x + 1)^2$: Graph moves to the left one unit.

  $y = (x - 1)^2$: Graph moves to the right one unit.

- $y = k \times f(x)$ stretches the original graph along the y axis by a factor of k.
  If $k > 1$, e.g. $y = 2x^2$, all the points are stretched upwards in the y direction by a scale factor of 2.
  If $k < 1$, e.g. $y = \frac{1}{2} x^2$, the graph is squashed downwards by a scale factor of $\frac{1}{2}$.

  The x values stay the same and the y values are multiplied by 2.

  The x values stay the same and the y values are multiplied by $\frac{1}{2}$.

- $y = f(k x)$ This is sometimes confusing.
  If $k > 1$, the graph stretches inwards in the x direction by $\frac{1}{k}$, e.g., if $y = (2x)^2$, the x coordinates are multiplied by $\frac{1}{2}$.
  If $k < 1$, the graph stretches outwards in the x direction by $\frac{1}{k}$, e.g., if $y = (\frac{1}{2}x)^2$, the x coordinates are multiplied by 2 ($1 \div \frac{1}{2} = 2$).

  The y coordinates stay the same and the x values are multiplied by $\frac{1}{2}$.

  The y coordinates stay the same and the x values are multiplied by 2.

QUICK TEST

1. Sketch these graphs:
   a) $y = x^3$ b) $y = x^3 - 4$ c) $y = (x - 2)^3$ d) $y = 2x^3$

2. Solve the simultaneous equations $y = x^2$ and $y = 3x + 4$.

Interpreting graphs

Distance–time graphs

These are often called **travel graphs**.
The **speed** of an object can be found by finding the gradient of the line.

$$\text{speed} = \frac{\text{distance travelled}}{\text{time taken}}$$

Example

The graph shows Mr Rogers' car journey. He set off at 9a.m. (0900).
Work out the speed of each stage.

a) The car is travelling at 30 m.p.h. for 1 hour (30 ÷ 1).
b) The car is stationary for 30 minutes.
c) The graph is steeper so the car is travelling faster, at a speed of 60 m.p.h. for 30 minutes (30 ÷ 0.5).
d) The car is stationary for 1 hour.
e) The return journey is at a speed of 40 m.p.h. (60 ÷ 1.5).

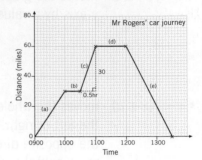

Mr Rogers' car journey

ℹ️ *Notice the importance of using the gradient of a line. It is useful to note that on the distance–time graph example, the scales on the axes are different. Care must be taken when reading the scales: always make sure you understand the scales before you start.*

Speed–time graphs

- A positive gradient means the speed is increasing.
- A negative gradient means the speed is decreasing.
- A horizontal line means the speed is constant.
- Distance is the area between the graph and the x axis.

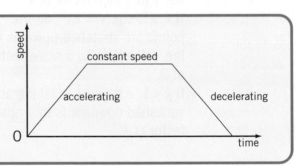

Using graphs to solve equations

A graph can be used to solve equations. Quite often the equation needs to be rearranged in order to resemble the equation of the plotted graph.

Example

The graph $y = x^2 - 2x + 1$ is drawn opposite.
Use the graph to solve the following equations:

a) $x^2 - 2x + 1 = 6$ b) $x^2 - 3x = 0$

a) $x^2 - 2x + 1 = 6$

Our graph is $y = x^2 - 2x + 1$. The solutions are where the line $y = 6$ crosses the graph:
$x = -1.45$, and $x = 3.45$

b) We need to rearrange the equation so it is like our graph:
$x^2 - 3x = 0$
$x^2 - 3x + x + 1 = x + 1$ Add $x + 1$ to both sides.
$x^2 - 2x + 1 = x + 1$

Our graph is $y = x^2 - 2x + 1$. The solutions are where the graph crosses the line $y = x + 1$:
$x = 0$ and $x = 3$.

$y = x^2 - 2x + 1$

$y = 6$

$y = x + 1$

Using graphs to find relationships

Sometimes you will be given a table of data which is known to fit a relationship.
If a suitable graph is drawn, the relationship can be found.

Example

The graph below is known to fit the relationship $y = pq^x$.
Use the graph to find the values of p and q and the relationship.

In order to find values for p and q, we need to take values at R and S,
then substitute them into the equation $y = pq^x$.

At point R, $x = 0$ and $y = 4$
so $\quad y = pq^x$ becomes
$\quad\quad 4 = p \times q^0 \quad$ Remember, $q^0 = 1$.
$\quad\quad 4 = p$

At point S, $x = 2$ and $y = 16$
So $\quad 16 = 4 \times q^2$
$\quad\quad 16 \div 4 = q^2 \quad$ Divide both sides by 4.
$\quad\quad\quad 4 = q^2$
$\quad\quad\quad q = \sqrt{4} = 2$

The relationship is $y = 4 \times 2^x$.

To find different coordinates on the graph, the $\boxed{x^y}$ button on the calculator is used.

When $x = 7$, $y = 4 \times 2^7 = 512$

N.B. You also need to revise work on **conversion graphs**.

KEY TERMS

Make sure you understand these terms before moving on!
- travel graph
- speed
- conversion graphs

❶

These containers are being filled with a liquid at a rate of 150 ml per second.
The graphs show how the depth of the water (d) changes with time (t).
Match the containers with the graphs.

❷ Draw the graph of $y = x^2 + x - 2$.
Use your graph to solve the following equations:

a) $x^2 + x = 5$
b) $x^2 - 2 = 0$
c) $x^2 - 2x - 2 = 0$

Practice questions

Use these questions to test your progress. Check your answers on page 109. You may wish to answer these questions on a separate piece of paper so that you can show full working out.

1. Solve the following equations:
   a) $2x + 4 = 10$ b) $3x - 1 = 11$ c) $5x - 3 = 2x + 12$ d) $3(x + 1) = 9$ e) $2(x + 1) = x + 3$

2. Here are the first five terms of a number sequence: 3, 9, 19, 33, 51.
   Write down an expression for the nth term of the sequence.

3. Simplify:
   a) $3x^2 \times 4x^2$
   b) $6x^2y \times 2x^3y^2$
   c) $12y^4 \div 3y$
   d) $(3y^2)^2$

4. Solve the simultaneous equations:
   $4a + 3b = 6$
   $2a - 3b = 12$

5. $p^2 = 5xy - 3x^2$ (C)
   a) Calculate the value of p when $x = 5.8$ and $y = 105$.
   b) Rearrange the formula $p^2 = 5xy - 3x^2$ to make y the subject.

6. The equation $x^3 - 2x = 2$ has a solution between 1 and 2.   (C)
   By using a method of trial and improvement, find this solution to 1 decimal place.

7. Solve the inequality $2 \leq 5n - 3 \leq 12$.

8. Match the graphs with the equations.
   a) $y = x^2 - 4$ b) $y = 2x + 1$ c) $y = 3 - 4x$ d) $xy = 6$

A   B   C   D

9. Simplify:
   a) $\dfrac{2}{(x + 4)} + \dfrac{3}{(x - 2)}$ b) $\dfrac{6}{x - 3} - \dfrac{2}{x + 4}$ c) $\dfrac{4a^2b}{a^4b} \times \dfrac{a^3b^2}{8ab^2}$

10. Factorise and then solve this quadratic equation: $2x^2 - 13x + 18 = 0$

(C) *Indicates that a calculator may be used.*

11. Solve these equations by using the quadratic formula:
    a) $3x^2 - 4x - 2 = 0$ b) $5x^2 - 3x - 1 = 0$ Ⓒ

    ....

12. Solve these equations by completing the square: Ⓒ
    a) $x^2 - 4x + 1 = 0$ ....
    b) $x^2 - 8x + 10 = 0$ ....

13. If the area of the rectangle is 50 cm²:
    a) Show that $x^2 + x - 27 = 0$.

    $(2x + 4)$ cm

    Area = 50 cm² $(x - 1)$ cm

    b) Work out the length of the rectangle.

    ....

14. Solve the simultaneous equations and interpret your solution geometrically.   Ⓒ
    $x^2 + y^2 = 16$ and $y = x + 4$

    ....

15. Make p the subject of the formula $6p + 2r = x(4 - p)$.

    ....

16. This is the graph of $y = f(x)$.
    On separate axes draw the graphs of:

    a) $y = f(x + 2)$
    b) $y = f(x) - 3$
    c) $y = -f(x)$
    d) $y = f(2x)$

    $y = f(x)$

17. This graph is known to fit the relationship $y = ab^x$ Ⓒ

    Use the graph to find the values of a and b.

    A (0,6)
    B (4,24)

    ....

Constructions and Plans

Plans and elevations

A **plan** is what is seen if a 3D shape is viewed from above.

An **elevation** is seen if the 3D shape is viewed from the side or front.

plan A

front elevation B

side elevation C

Constructing a triangle

Example
Use compasses to construct this triangle.
- Draw the longest side.
- With the compass point at A, draw an arc of radius 4 cm.
- With the compass point at B, draw an arc of radius 5 cm.
- Join A and B to the point where the two arcs meet at C.

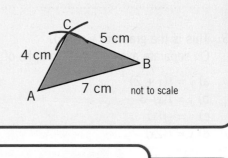

4 cm 5 cm 7 cm not to scale

The perpendicular bisector of a line segment

Construct the **perpendicular bisector** of the **line segment** XY.
- Draw two arcs with the compasses, using X as the centre. The compasses must be set at a radius greater than half the distance of XY.
- Draw two more arcs with Y as the centre.
  (Keep the compasses the same distance apart as before.)
- Join the two points where the arcs cross.
- AB is the **perpendicular bisector** of XY.
- N is the **midpoint** of XY.

The perpendicular from a point to a line

Construct the perpendicular from point P to the line AB.
- From P draw arcs to cut the line at A and B.
- From A and B draw arcs with the same radius to intersect at a point C below the line.
- Join P to C; this line is perpendicular to AB.

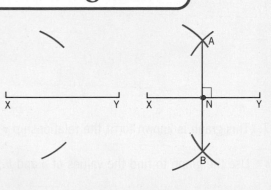

The perpendicular from a point on a straight line

Construct the perpendicular at the point N on a line.
- With the compasses set to a radius of about 4 cm, and centred on N, draw arcs to cut the line at A and B.
- Construct the **perpendicular bisector** of the line segment AB as above.

Bisecting an angle

- Draw two lines XY and YZ to meet at an angle.
- Using compasses, place the point at Y and draw the two arcs on XY and YZ.
- Place the compass point at the two arcs on XY and YZ and draw arcs to cross at N.
- Join Y and N. YN is the **bisector** of angle XYZ.

Construction of an inscribed regular polygon

Example
Construct a regular hexagon inside a circle of radius 2 cm.

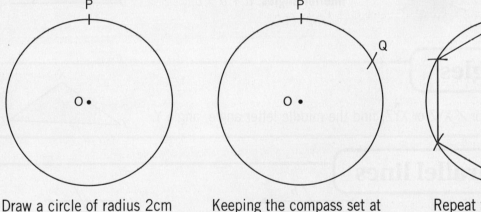

Draw a circle of radius 2cm and mark a point P on its circumference.

Keeping the compass set at 2 cm, draw an arc, centre P, which cuts the circle at Q. Q is the centre of the next arc.

Repeat the process until six points are marked on the circumference. Join the points to make a hexagon.

QUICK TEST

1. Bisect this angle.
2. Draw the perpendicular bisector of a 10 cm line.

Angles

An *acute angle* is between 0° and 90°.

An *obtuse angle* is between 90° and 180°.

A *reflex angle* is between 180° and 360°.

A right angle is 90°.

Angle facts

Angles on a straight line add up to **180°**.
$a + b + c = 180°$

Angles at a point add up to **360°**.
$a + b + c + d = 360°$

Angles in a triangle add up to **180°**.
$a + b + c = 180°$

Angles in a quadrilateral add up to **360°**.
$a + b + c + d = 360°$

Vertically opposite angles are **equal**.
$a = b, c = d$
$a + d = b + c = 180°$

An **exterior angle** of a triangle equals the sum of the **two opposite interior angles**. $a + b = c$

Reading angles

When asked to find XYZ or ∠XYZ or XŶZ, find the middle letter angle, angle Y.

Angles in parallel lines

Alternate (z) angles are **equal**.

Corresponding angles are **equal**.

Supplementary angles add up to **180°**: $c + d = 180°$

Examples
Find the angles labelled by letters.

$a = 50° + 70°$
$a = 120°$

$a + 80° + 40° + 85° = 360°$
$a = 360° - 205°$
$\quad = 155°$

$a = 120°$ (angles on a straight line)
$b = 60°$ (vertically opposite to 60°)
$c = 60°$ (corresponding to b or alternate to 60°)
$d = 60°$ (vertically opposite to c)

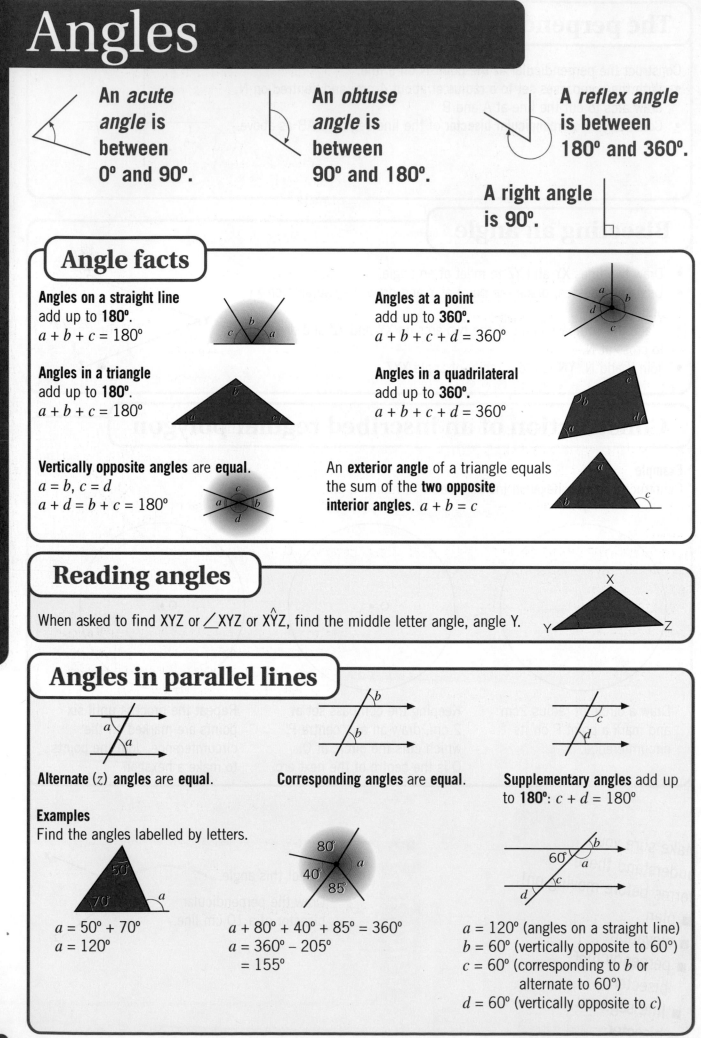

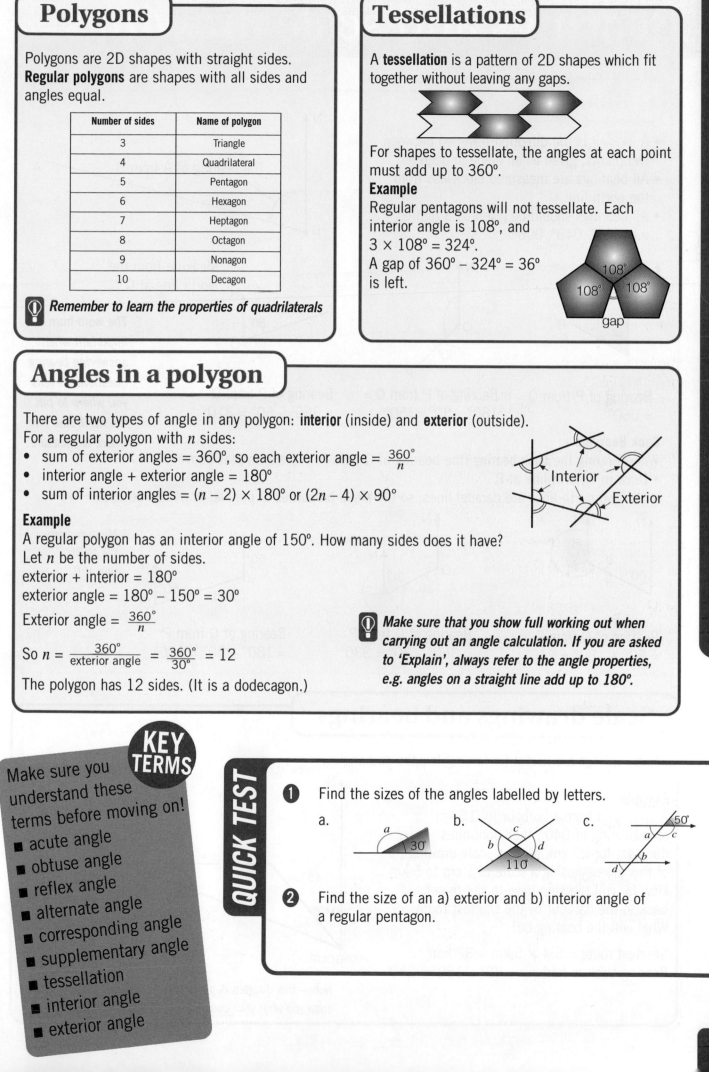

Polygons

Polygons are 2D shapes with straight sides.
Regular polygons are shapes with all sides and angles equal.

Number of sides	Name of polygon
3	Triangle
4	Quadrilateral
5	Pentagon
6	Hexagon
7	Heptagon
8	Octagon
9	Nonagon
10	Decagon

💡 *Remember to learn the properties of quadrilaterals*

Tessellations

A **tessellation** is a pattern of 2D shapes which fit together without leaving any gaps.

For shapes to tessellate, the angles at each point must add up to 360°.
Example
Regular pentagons will not tessellate. Each interior angle is 108°, and
$3 \times 108° = 324°$.
A gap of $360° - 324° = 36°$ is left.

108°
108°   108°
gap

Angles in a polygon

There are two types of angle in any polygon: **interior** (inside) and **exterior** (outside).
For a regular polygon with n sides:
- sum of exterior angles = 360°, so each exterior angle = $\frac{360°}{n}$
- interior angle + exterior angle = 180°
- sum of interior angles = $(n - 2) \times 180°$ or $(2n - 4) \times 90°$

Interior

Exterior

Example
A regular polygon has an interior angle of 150°. How many sides does it have?
Let n be the number of sides.
exterior + interior = 180°
exterior angle = 180° - 150° = 30°

Exterior angle = $\frac{360°}{n}$

So $n = \frac{360°}{\text{exterior angle}} = \frac{360°}{30°} = 12$

The polygon has 12 sides. (It is a dodecagon.)

💡 *Make sure that you show full working out when carrying out an angle calculation. If you are asked to 'Explain', always refer to the angle properties, e.g. angles on a straight line add up to 180°.*

KEY TERMS

Make sure you understand these terms before moving on!
- acute angle
- obtuse angle
- reflex angle
- alternate angle
- corresponding angle
- supplementary angle
- tessellation
- interior angle
- exterior angle

QUICK TEST

1. Find the sizes of the angles labelled by letters.

a.
a
30°

b.
c
b d
110°

c.
50°
a c
b
d

2. Find the size of an a) exterior and b) interior angle of a regular pentagon.

Bearings and scale drawings

Bearings

- A **bearing** is the direction travelled between two points, given as an angle in degrees.
- All bearings are measured clockwise from the north line.
- All bearings should be given as 3 figures, e.g. 225°, 043°, 006°.

The bearing of A from B

Examples

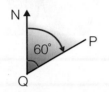

Bearing of P from Q = 060°

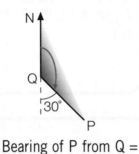

Bearing of P from Q = 180° − 30° =150°

Bearing of P from Q = 360° − 50° = 310°

Measure from the North line at Q.

> 💡 *The word from is important when answering bearing questions. It tells you where to put the north line and where to measure.*

Back Bearings

When finding the **back bearing** (the bearing of Q from P in the examples above):
- Draw in a north line at P.
- The two north lines are parallel lines, so the angle properties of parallel lines can be used.

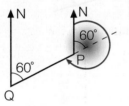

Bearing of Q from P = 60° + 180° = 240°

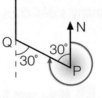

Bearing of Q from P = 360° − 30° = 330°

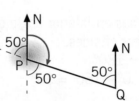

Bearing of Q from P = 180° − 50° = 130°

Measure from the North line at P.

Scale drawings and bearings

Scale drawings are useful for finding lengths and angles.

Example
A ship sails from a harbour for 15 km on a bearing of 040°, then continues due east for 20 km. Make a scale drawing of this journey using a scale of 1 cm to 5 km. How far will the ship have to sail to get back to the harbour by the shortest route? What will the bearing be?

Shortest route = 6.4 × 5 km = 32 km
Bearing back to harbour = 70° + 180° = 250°

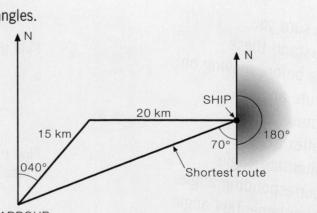

Note – this diagram is not drawn accurately but is used to show you what your diagram should look like.

Scales and maps

Scales are often used on maps. They are usually written as a ratio.

Example

The scale on a road map is 1 : 25000. Bury and Oldham are 20 cm apart on the map.
Work out the real distance, in km, between Bury and Oldham.

Scale 1 : 25000, distance on map is 20 cm.
∴ Real distance = 20 × 25000 = 500000 cm
Divide by 100 to change cm to m:
    500000 ÷ 100 = 5000 m
Divide by 1000 to change m to km:
    5000 ÷ 1000 = 5 km

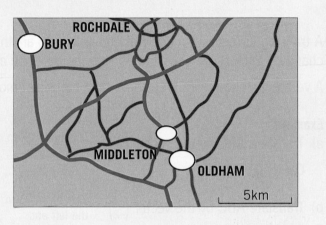

A scale of 1 : 25000 means that 1 cm on the scale drawing represents a real length of 25000 cm.

KEY TERMS

Make sure you understand these terms before moving on!
■ bearing
■ scale drawing

QUICK TEST

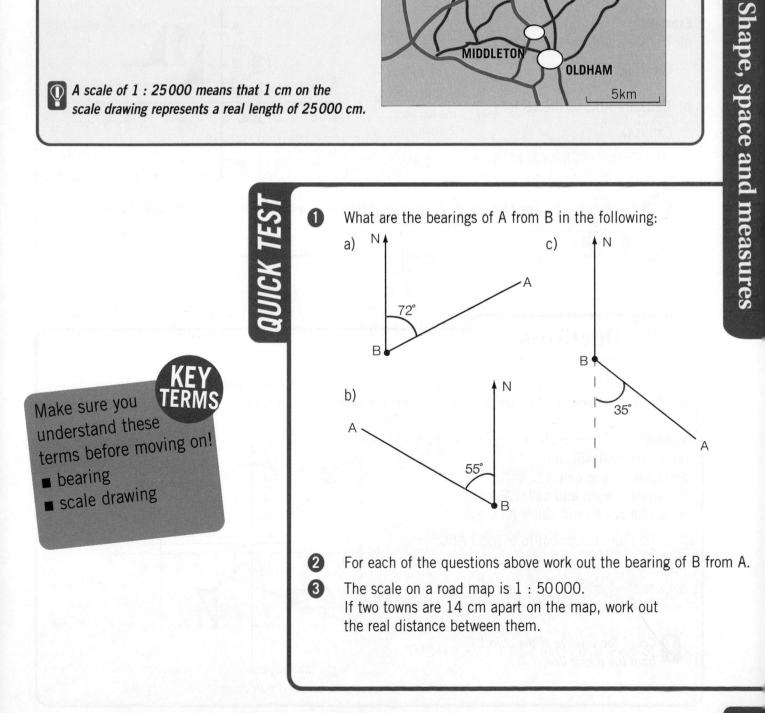

1 What are the bearings of A from B in the following:

a) 72°

b) 55°

c) 35°

2 For each of the questions above work out the bearing of B from A.

3 The scale on a road map is 1 : 50000.
If two towns are 14 cm apart on the map, work out the real distance between them.

Transformations 1

A transformation changes the position or size of a shape.
There are four types of transformations:
translations, *reflections*, *rotations* and *enlargements*.

Translations

A translation moves a figure from one place to another. The size and shape of the figure are not changed. **Vectors** are used to describe the distance and direction of a translation.

A vector is written $\binom{a}{b}$. a represents the **horizontal** movement, and b represents the **vertical** movement.

Example

a) Translate ABC by the vector $\binom{2}{1}$.

Call it P.

This means 2 to the right and 1 upwards.

b) Translate ABC by the vector $\binom{-3}{-2}$.

Call it Q.

This means 3 to the left and 2 down.

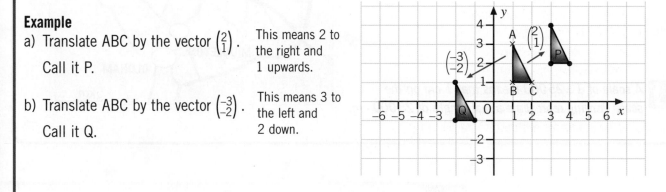

P and Q are **congruent** – two shapes are congruent if they have exactly the same size and shape.

Reflections

A reflection creates an image of an object on the other side of the **mirror line**. The mirror line is known as an **axis of reflection**. The size and shape of the figure are not changed.

Example

Reflect triangle ABC in:
a) the *x* axis, and call it D;
b) the line $y = -x$, and call it E;
c) the line $x = 5$, and call it F.

D, E and F are congruent to triangle ABC.

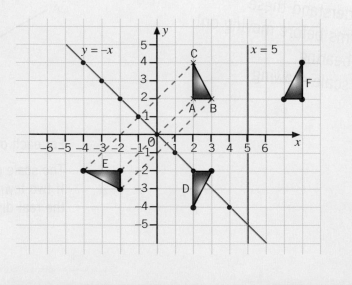

> Count the squares of the object from the mirror line.

Rotations

A rotation turns a figure through an angle about some fixed point. This fixed point is called the **centre of rotation**. The size and shape of the figure are not changed.

Example

Rotate triangle ABC:

a) 90° clockwise about (0, 0) and call it R;

b) 180° about (0, 0), and call it S;

c) 90° anticlockwise about (–1, 1), and call it T.

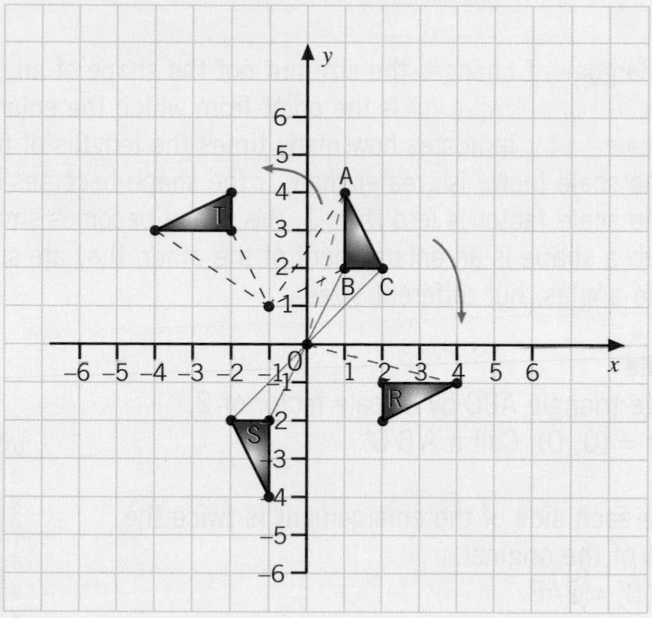

When describing a rotation give:
- *the centre of rotation*
- *the direction of the turn (clockwise or anticlockwise)*
- *the angle of the turn*

If you don't give all 3 pieces of information, you will lose marks for not describing them fully.

KEY TERMS

Make sure you understand these terms before moving on!
- translation
- reflection
- rotation
- enlargement
- vector
- congruent

1 On the diagram below:

a) Translate triangle ABC by the vector $\begin{pmatrix} -3 \\ 1 \end{pmatrix}$. Call it P.

b) Reflect ABC in the line $y = x$. Call it Q.

c) Reflect ABC in the line $y = -1$. Call it R.

d) Rotate ABC 180° about (0, 0). Call it S.

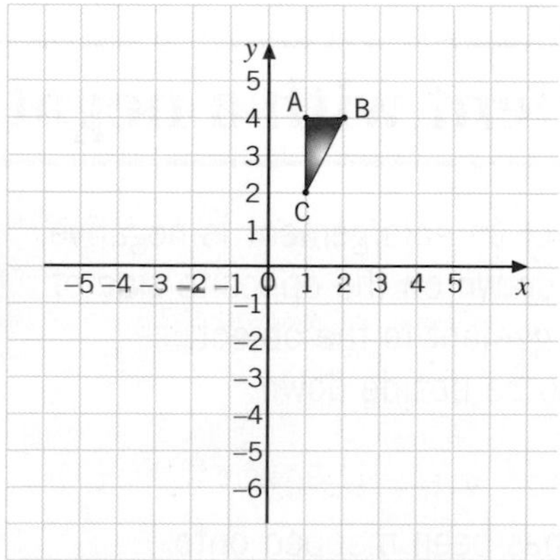

2 What does the vector $\begin{pmatrix} -2 \\ 3 \end{pmatrix}$ mean?

61

Transformations 2

Enlargements

An enlargement changes the size but not the shape of an object.
The **centre of enlargement** is the point from which the enlargement takes place.
The **scale factor** indicates how many times the lengths of the original figure have increased in size.
- If the scale factor is greater than 1, the shape becomes bigger.
- If the scale factor is less than 1, the shape becomes smaller.
- When a shape is an enlargement of the other, they are similar, i.e. they are the same shape with the same angles, but different sizes.

Example
Enlarge triangle ABC by a scale factor of 2,
centre = (0, 0). Call it A'B'C'.

Notice each side of the enlargement is twice the length of the original.
e.g. A'B' = 2AB

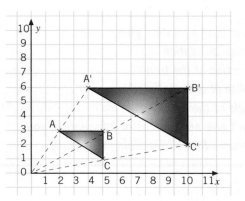

Example
Describe fully the transformation that maps
ABCDEF onto A'B'C'D'E'F'.
- To find the centre of enlargement, join A to A', and continue the line. Join B to B', and continue the line. Do the same for the others.
- Where all the lines meet is the centre of enlargement: (–1, 3).
- The transformation is an enlargement with scale factor $\frac{1}{3}$ and centre of enlargement at (–1, 3).

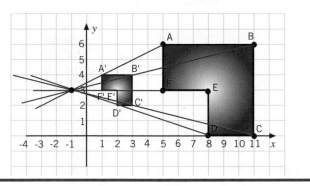

Enlargement with a negative scale factor

If the scale factor of an enlargement is negative, then the image is drawn on the opposite side of the centre of enlargement to the object.
The image will also be upside down.

Example
The triangle ABC has been mapped onto
$A_1B_1C_1$ by a scale factor of –2,
centre at 0.

💡 *When asked to describe an enlargement, you must include both the scale factor and the position of the centre of enlargement.*

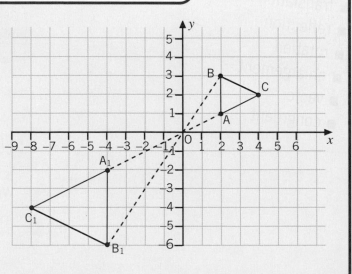

Combining transformations

Transformations can be combined in a series
of two or more transformations.

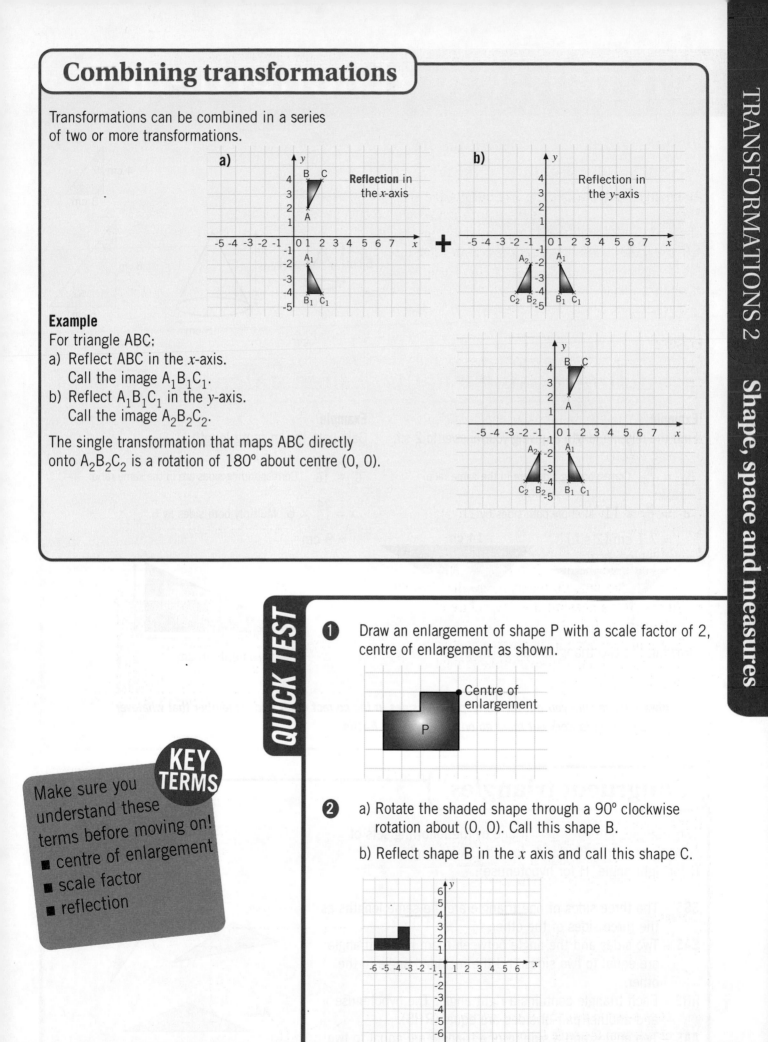

Example

For triangle ABC:

a) Reflect ABC in the *x*-axis.
   Call the image $A_1B_1C_1$.

b) Reflect $A_1B_1C_1$ in the *y*-axis.
   Call the image $A_2B_2C_2$.

The single transformation that maps ABC directly
onto $A_2B_2C_2$ is a rotation of 180° about centre (0, 0).

QUICK TEST

1 Draw an enlargement of shape P with a scale factor of 2,
centre of enlargement as shown.

• Centre of
enlargement

P

2 a) Rotate the shaded shape through a 90° clockwise
rotation about (0, 0). Call this shape B.

b) Reflect shape B in the *x* axis and call this shape C.

Similarity and congruency

Similar figures are those which are the same shape but different sizes. Corresponding angles are equal. Corresponding lengths are in the same ratio.

Notice corresponding lengths are in the same ratio. The lengths of the bigger cone are twice those of the smaller cone.

Examples

Corresponding angles are equal.

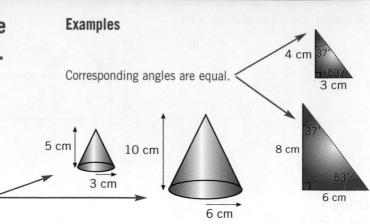

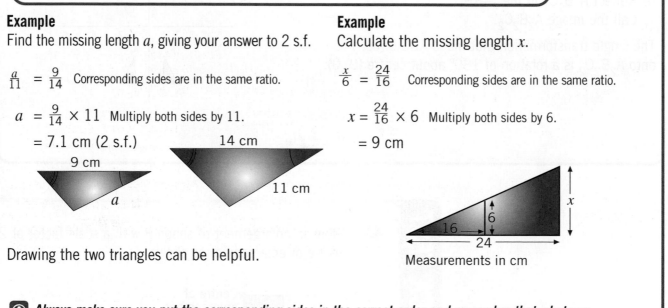

Finding missing lengths of similar figures

Example

Find the missing length a, giving your answer to 2 s.f.

$\frac{a}{11} = \frac{9}{14}$ Corresponding sides are in the same ratio.

$a = \frac{9}{14} \times 11$ Multiply both sides by 11.

$= 7.1$ cm (2 s.f.)

Drawing the two triangles can be helpful.

Example

Calculate the missing length x.

$\frac{x}{6} = \frac{24}{16}$ Corresponding sides are in the same ratio.

$x = \frac{24}{16} \times 6$ Multiply both sides by 6.

$= 9$ cm

Measurements in cm

💡 *Always make sure you put the corresponding sides in the correct order and remember that whatever you are trying to work out must go on the top of the fraction.*

Congruent triangles

Two triangles are **congruent** if one of the following sets of conditions is true (S stands for side, A for angle, R for right angle, H for hypotenuse):

SSS – The three sides of one triangle are the same lengths as the three sides of the other.

SAS – Two sides and the angle between them in one triangle are equal to two sides and the included angle in the other.

RHS – Each triangle contains a right angle. The hypotenuse and another pair of sides are equal (RHS).

AAS – Two angles and a side in one triangle are equal to two angles and the corresponding side in the other.

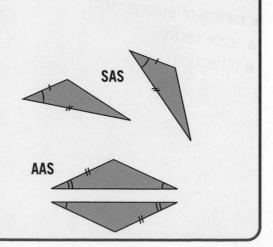

Area and volumes of similar figures

Areas of similar figures are not in the same ratio as their lengths. For example, the corresponding lengths of these squares are in the ratio 1 : 2 but their areas are in the ratio 1 : 4.
If the corresponding lengths are in the ratio $a : b$, their areas are in the ratio $a^2 : b^2$.
A similar result can be found when looking at the volumes of similar objects: if the corresponding lengths are in the ratio $a : b$, their volumes are in the ratio $a^3 : b^3$.

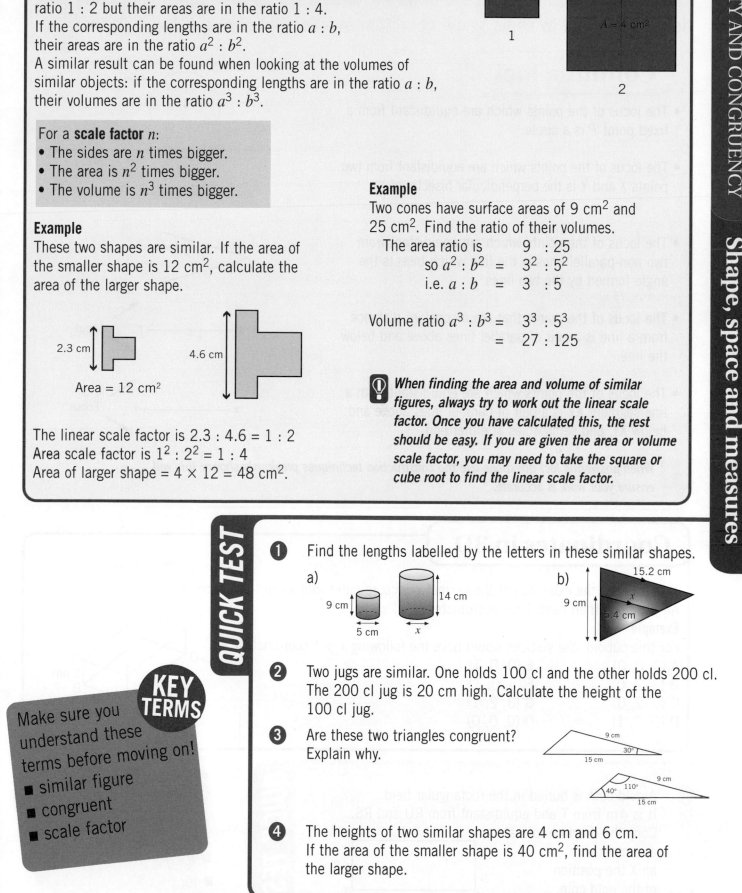

$A = 1$ cm^2

$A = 4$ cm^2

1

2

For a scale factor n:
- The sides are n times bigger.
- The area is n^2 times bigger.
- The volume is n^3 times bigger.

Example
These two shapes are similar. If the area of the smaller shape is 12 cm^2, calculate the area of the larger shape.

2.3 cm

4.6 cm

Area = 12 cm^2

The linear scale factor is 2.3 : 4.6 = 1 : 2
Area scale factor is $1^2 : 2^2$ = 1 : 4
Area of larger shape = 4 × 12 = 48 cm^2.

Example
Two cones have surface areas of 9 cm^2 and 25 cm^2. Find the ratio of their volumes.

	The area ratio is	9	:	25
	so $a^2 : b^2$ =	3^2	:	5^2
	i.e. $a : b$ =	3	:	5

Volume ratio $a^3 : b^3$ = 3^3 : 5^3
=   27 : 125

ⓘ *When finding the area and volume of similar figures, always try to work out the linear scale factor. Once you have calculated this, the rest should be easy. If you are given the area or volume scale factor, you may need to take the square or cube root to find the linear scale factor.*

① Find the lengths labelled by the letters in these similar shapes.

a)

9 cm   14 cm

5 cm x

b)

15.2 cm

9 cm x

5.4 cm

② Two jugs are similar. One holds 100 cl and the other holds 200 cl. The 200 cl jug is 20 cm high. Calculate the height of the 100 cl jug.

KEY TERMS

Make sure you understand these terms before moving on!
- similar figure
- congruent
- scale factor

③ Are these two triangles congruent? Explain why.

9 cm

30°

15 cm

9 cm

40°   110°

15 cm

④ The heights of two similar shapes are 4 cm and 6 cm. If the area of the smaller shape is 40 cm^2, find the area of the larger shape.

Loci and coordinates in 3D

The *locus* of a point is the set of all the possible positions which that point can occupy, subject to some given condition or rule. The plural of locus is *loci*.

Common loci

- The locus of the points which are equidistant from a fixed point *P* is a circle.

- The locus of the points which are equidistant from two points X and Y is the perpendicular bisector of XY.

- The locus of the points which are equidistant from two non-parallel lines is the line which bisects the angle formed by the two lines.

- The locus of the points that are a constant distance from a line is a pair of parallel lines above and below the line.

- The locus of the points which are equidistant from a line segment XY is a pair of parallel lines above and below XY, and semicircles at either end.

When answering loci questions use the construction techniques previously shown: this will ensure your work is accurate.

Coordinates in 3D

This involves the extension of the normal x–y coordinates into a third direction, known as z. All positions then have three coordinates (x, y, z).

Example

For this cuboid, the vertices would have the following x–y–z coordinates:

A (3, 0, 0)   E (0, 0, 1)
B (3, 2, 0)   F (3, 0, 1)
C (0, 2, 0)   G (3, 2, 1)
D (0, 2, 1)   O (0, 0, 0)

QUICK TEST

① A gold coin is buried in the rectangular field.
It is 4 m from T and equidistant from RU and RS.
Copy the diagram to scale and mark with an X the position of the gold coin.

R —— 5 m —— S
2 m
U —— T
Scale 1 cm : 1 m

KEY TERMS

Make sure you understand these terms before moving on!

- locus
- loci

Angle properties of circles

Circle theorems

There are several circle theorems you need to know and be able to apply. The theorems are:

1. The **perpendicular bisector** of any chord passes through the centre.

2. The angle in a semicircle is always 90°.

3. The radius and a **tangent** always meet at 90°.

4. Angles in the same **segment** are equal,
e.g. $\hat{ABC} = \hat{ADC}$

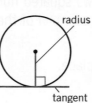

5. The angle at the centre is twice the angle at the circumference,
e.g. $\hat{POQ} = 2 \times \hat{PRQ}$

6. Opposite angles of a **cyclic quadrilateral** add up to 180°. (A cyclic quadrilateral is a 4-sided shape with each corner touching the circumference of the circle) i.e. $x + y = 180°$
$$a + b = 180°$$

7. The lengths of two tangents from a point are equal,
e.g. RS = RT

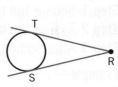

8. The angle between a tangent and a **chord** is equal to the angle in the alternate segment (that is, the angle which is made at the edge of the circle by two lines drawn from the chord).
This is known as the **Alternate Segment Theorem**.
i.e. $a = b$

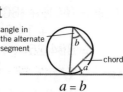

angle in the alternate segment

chord

$a = b$

> It is very important that you learn all of these eight theorems and that you can apply and explain them.

KEY TERMS

Make sure you understand these terms before moving on!
- perpendicular bisector
- tangent
- segment
- cyclic quadrilateral
- chord
- alternate segment theorem

QUICK TEST

❶ Calculate the missing angles in the diagram below and state which circle theorems you are using.

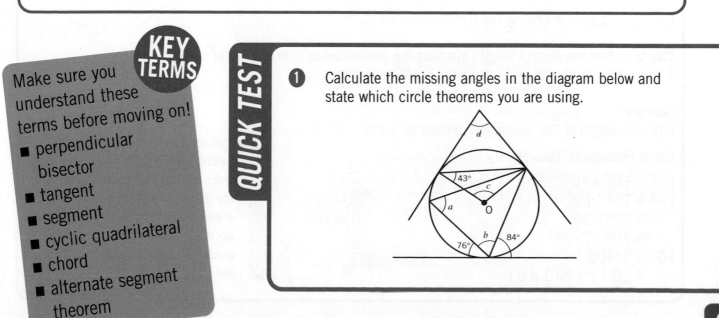

Pythagoras' theorem

Pythagoras' theorem states: in any right-angled triangle, the square on the
hypotenuse **is equal to the sum of the squares on the other two sides.**
The hypotenuse is the longest side of a right-angled triangle.
It is always opposite the right angle.

Using the letters in the diagram, the theorem is written as:
$$c^2 = a^2 + b^2$$
This can be rearranged to give $a^2 = c^2 - b^2$ or $b^2 = c^2 - a^2$.
These forms are useful when calculating the length of one of the shorter sides.

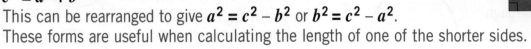

Finding the length of the hypotenuse

Remember: Pythagoras' theorem can only be used for right-angled triangles.

Step 1 Square the two lengths of the two shorter sides that you are given.
Step 2 To find the hypotenuse (longest side) add these two squared numbers.
Step 3 After adding the two squared lengths, take the **square root** of the sum.

Example
Find the length of AB, giving your answer to 1 decimal place.

Using Pythagoras' theorem:

$(AB)^2 = (AC)^2 + (BC)^2$
$\quad\quad\quad = 12^2 + 14.5^2$
$\quad\quad\quad = 354.25$

$AB \quad = \sqrt{354.25}$ Take the square root to find AB.
$\quad\quad\quad = 18.8$ m (to 1 d.p.)   Round to 1 d.p.

Finding the length of a shorter side

Follow the steps for finding the hypotenuse except:

Step 2 To find the shorter length, subtract the smaller value from the larger value.
• Remember to take the square root ($\sqrt{\ }$) of your answer.

Example
Find the length of FG, giving your answer to 1 d.p.

Using Pythagoras' theorem:

$EF^2 = EG^2 + FG^2$
$FG^2 = EF^2 - EG^2$
$\quad\quad = 27^2 - 18^2$
$\quad\quad = 405$
$FG \quad = \sqrt{405}$
$\quad\quad = 20.1$ cm (to 1 d.p.)

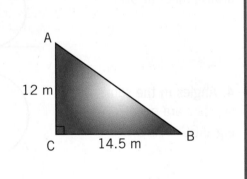

💡 *Pythagoras' theorem allows us to
calculate the length of one of the
sides of a right-angled triangle, when
the other two sides are known.*
*If you are not told to what degree of
accuracy to round your answer, be
guided by significant figures given in
the question.*

Calculating the length of a line AB, given two sets of coordinates

By drawing in a triangle between the two points A (1, 2) and B (7, 6) we can find the length of AB by Pythagoras' theorem.

Horizontal distance = 6   (7 − 1)
Vertical distance = 4   (6 − 2)
Length of $(AB)^2 = 6^2 + 4^2$
$= 36 + 16$
$= 52$
$AB = \sqrt{52}$
Length of AB = 7.21 (to 2 d.p.)

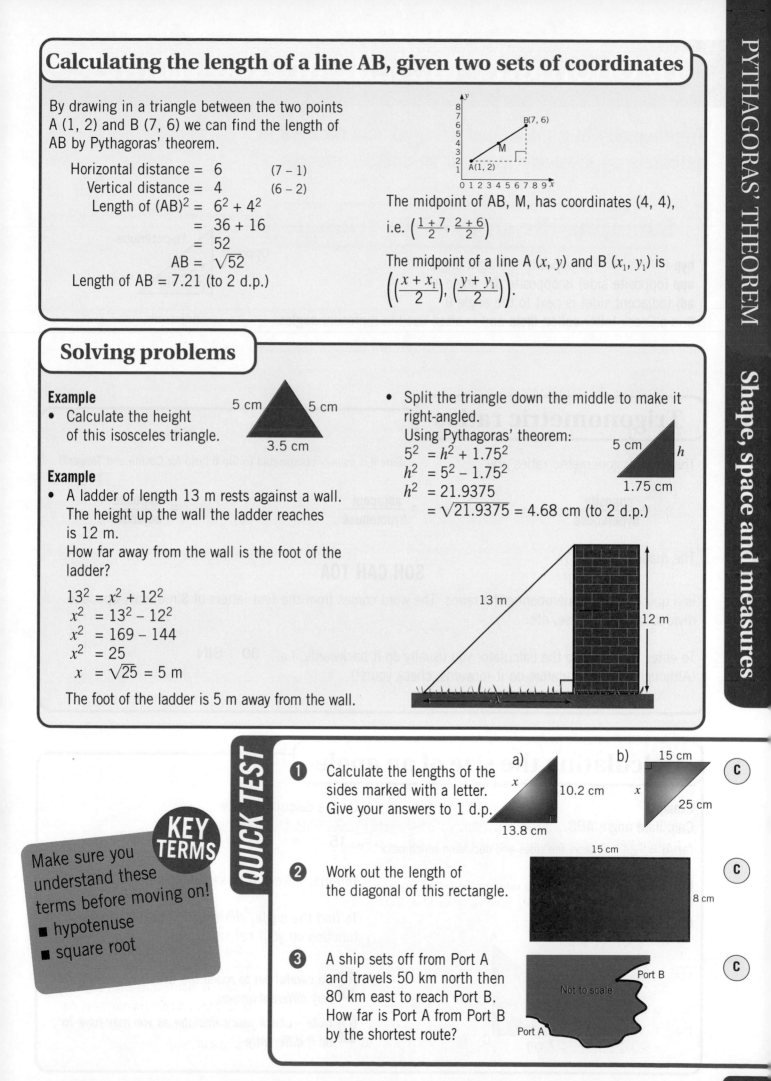

The midpoint of AB, M, has coordinates (4, 4),
i.e. $\left(\frac{1+7}{2}, \frac{2+6}{2}\right)$

The midpoint of a line A (x, y) and B (x_1, y_1) is
$\left(\left(\frac{x + x_1}{2}\right), \left(\frac{y + y_1}{2}\right)\right)$.

Solving problems

Example
• Calculate the height of this isosceles triangle.

5 cm   5 cm
3.5 cm

Example
• A ladder of length 13 m rests against a wall. The height up the wall the ladder reaches is 12 m.
How far away from the wall is the foot of the ladder?

$13^2 = x^2 + 12^2$
$x^2 = 13^2 - 12^2$
$x^2 = 169 - 144$
$x^2 = 25$
$x = \sqrt{25} = 5$ m

The foot of the ladder is 5 m away from the wall.

• Split the triangle down the middle to make it right-angled.
Using Pythagoras' theorem:
$5^2 = h^2 + 1.75^2$
$h^2 = 5^2 - 1.75^2$
$h^2 = 21.9375$
$= \sqrt{21.9375} = 4.68$ cm (to 2 d.p.)

5 cm   h
1.75 cm

13 m   12 m

QUICK TEST

1 Calculate the lengths of the sides marked with a letter. Give your answers to 1 d.p.   **C**

a)
x 10.2 cm
13.8 cm

b)   15 cm
x 25 cm

2 Work out the length of the diagonal of this rectangle.   **C**

15 cm
8 cm

3 A ship sets off from Port A and travels 50 km north then 80 km east to reach Port B. How far is Port A from Port B by the shortest route?   **C**

Port B
Not to scale
Port A

Trigonometry in right-angled triangles

Trigonometry in right-angled triangles can be used to calculate an unknown angle or an unknown length.

Labelling the sides of the triangle

hyp (**hypotenuse**) is opposite the right angle.
opp (**opposite side**) is opposite the angle θ.
adj (**adjacent side**) is next to the angle θ.
θ is a Greek letter called **theta** and is often used to represent **angles**.

Trigonometric ratios

The three trigonometric ratios are:

Sine θ is usually abbreviated to Sin θ (also for Cosine and Tangent)

$$\text{Sin } \theta = \frac{\text{opposite}}{\text{hypotenuse}} \qquad \text{Cos } \theta = \frac{\text{adjacent}}{\text{hypotenuse}} \qquad \text{Tan } \theta = \frac{\text{opposite}}{\text{adjacent}}$$

The made-up word

SOH CAH TOA

is a quick way of remembering the ratios. The word comes from the first letters of **S**in equals **O**pposite divided by **H**ypotenuse, etc.

To enter 'sin 30' into the calculator you usually do it backwards, i.e. [30] [SIN].
(Although some calculators do it forwards: check yours!)

Calculating the size of an angle

Example
Calculate angle ABC.

$\tan \theta = \frac{\text{opp}}{\text{adj}}$ Label the sides and decide on which ratio you need.

$\tan \theta = \frac{15}{27}$ Divide the top value by the bottom value.

$\tan \theta = 0.\dot{5}$
$\theta = 29.1°$ (1 d.p.)

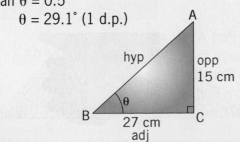

On the calculator, type:

[15] [÷] [27] [=] [inv] [tan] [=]

You may have a shift key on your calculator.

To find the angle, you usually use the second function on your calculator.

🕮 *Be careful not to round 0.5̇ to 0.6 as you will get a very different answer.*

🕮 *Note – check your calculator as you may have to do it differently.*

Calculating the length of a side

Example
Calculate the length of BC.
• Label the sides first.
• Decide on the ratio.

$$\sin 30° = \frac{opp}{hyp}$$

• Substitute in the values you have been given.

$$\sin 30° = \frac{BC}{25}$$

$25 \times \sin 30° = BC$ Multiply both sides by 25.
$BC = 12.5$ cm

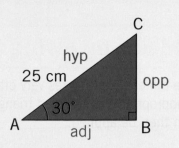

💡 *When calculating the size of an angle it should usually be rounded to 1 d.p. However, do not round off your answer until right at the end of the question.*
You must learn the trigonometric ratios as they are no longer on the formula sheets.

Example
Calculate the length of EF.

$$\cos 40° = \frac{adj}{hyp} = \frac{20}{EF}$$

$EF \times \cos 40° = 20$ Multiply both sides by EF.
$EF = \dfrac{20}{\cos 40°}$ Divide both sides by cos 40°.
    $= 26.1$ cm (1 d.p.)

On a calculator, key: | 20 | ÷ | 40 | cos | = | or | 20 | ÷ | cos | 40 | = |

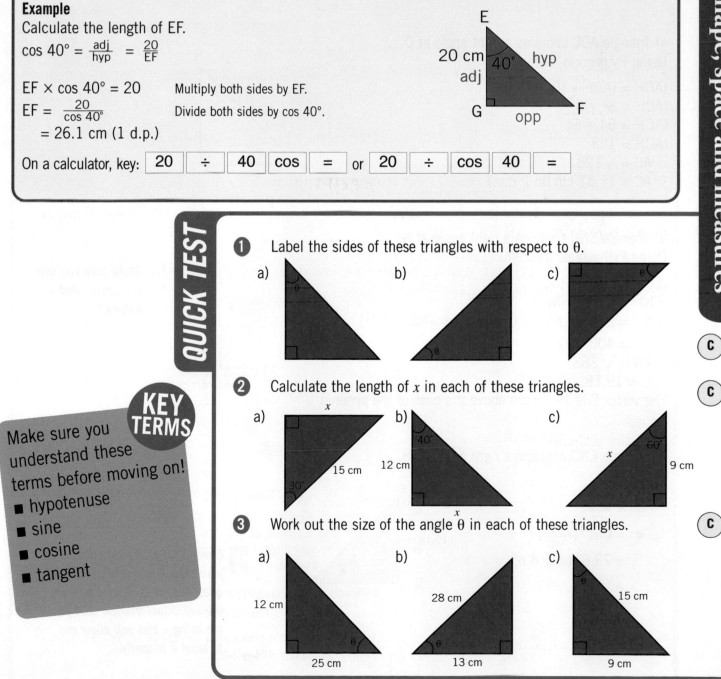

QUICK TEST

1 Label the sides of these triangles with respect to θ.
a)   b)   c)

2 Calculate the length of *x* in each of these triangles.
a)   b)   c)

3 Work out the size of the angle θ in each of these triangles.
a)   b)   c)

KEY TERMS

Make sure you understand these terms before moving on!
■ hypotenuse
■ sine
■ cosine
■ tangent

71

Application of trigonometry

Solving problems involving three-dimensional figures

Problems involving three-dimensional figures very often have to be broken down into several stages. It is essential that the appropriate right-angled triangles are identified. The trigonometric ratios and Pythagoras' theorem can then be applied.

Example

The diagram shows a square-based pyramid.
The point E lies directly above N.
N is the midpoint of the base.

a) Calculate the distance AC.
b) Calculate the height of the vertex E above the base.
c) Calculate the angle between EC and the base ABCD.

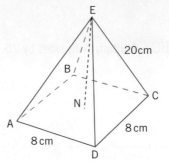

a) Triangle ADC contains a right angle at D.
Using Pythagoras' theorem:

$(AC)^2 = (AD)^2 + (DC)^2$
$(AC)^2 = 8^2 + 8^2$
$(AC)^2 = 64 + 64$
$(AC)^2 = 128$
$\quad AC = \sqrt{128}$
$\quad AC = 11.31$ cm (to 2 d.p.)

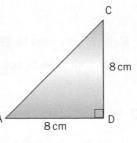

b) Triangle ENC contains a right angle at N.
Using Pythagoras' theorem:

$(EC)^2 = (EN)^2 + (NC)^2$
$(EN)^2 = (EC)^2 - (NC)^2$
$(EN)^2 = 20^2 - 5.65^2...$ (Since NC $= \frac{1}{2}AC = \frac{11.31}{2}$)
$(EN)^2 = 400 - 32$
$\quad EN = \sqrt{368}$
$\qquad = 19.18...$ cm
The vertex E is 19.18 cm above the base of the pyramid.

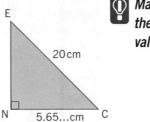

> ❗ **Make sure you use the unrounded values.**

c) Triangle ENC contains a right angle at N.

$\text{Cos } \theta = \frac{adj}{hyp}$
$\qquad = \frac{5.65...}{20}$
$\quad \theta = \text{Cos}^{-1}(\frac{5.65...}{20})$
$\qquad = 73.6°$ (to 1 d.p.)

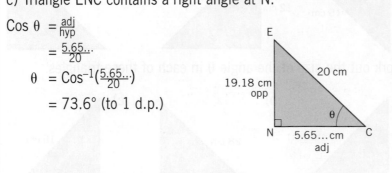

> ❗ **Check that you know how to use your calculator for trigonometry questions. It is helpful to draw the individual triangle that you are using – this will allow you to label it properly.**

Angles of elevation and depression

The **angle of elevation** is measured from the horizontal **upwards**.

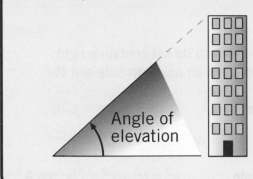

Angle of elevation

The **angle of depression** is measured from the horizontal **downwards**.

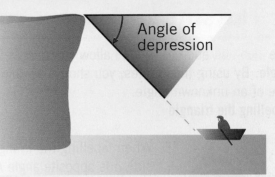

Angle of depression

Bearings and Trigonometry

Example

In the diagram, A, B and C represent three towns. The distance AB is 16km. The distance BC is 9km.

Work out the bearing of B from A.

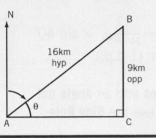

The required bearing is from the North at A. Find angle A.

$\text{Sin } \theta = \frac{\text{opp}}{\text{hyp}}$

$\text{Sin } \theta = \frac{9}{16}$

$\theta = \text{Sin}^{-1} \frac{9}{16}$

$= 34.2°$ (to 1d.p.)

Bearing of B from A is $90° - 34.2° = 55.8°$

KEY TERMS

Make sure you understand these terms before moving on!
- angle of elevation
- angle of depression

QUICK TEST

1 Dipak stands 30 m from the base of a tower. He measures the angle of elevation from ground level to the top of the tower as 50°. Calculate the height of the tower. Give your answer to 3 s.f. **C**

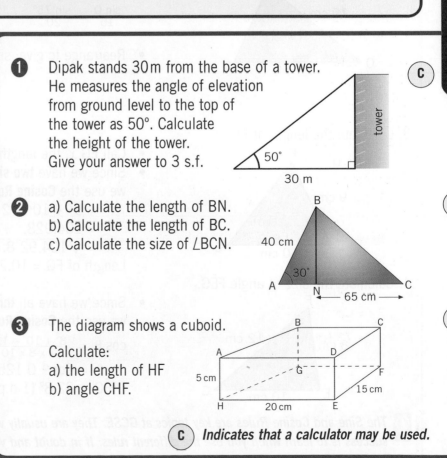

2 a) Calculate the length of BN.
b) Calculate the length of BC.
c) Calculate the size of ∠BCN. **C**

3 The diagram shows a cuboid.
Calculate:
a) the length of HF
b) angle CHF. **C**

C *Indicates that a calculator may be used.*

73

Further trigonometry

The sine and cosine rules

The **sine rule** and **cosine rule** allow you to solve problems in triangles which do not contain a right angle. By using these rules, you should be able to calculate the length of an unknown side and the size of an unknown angle.

Labelling the triangle

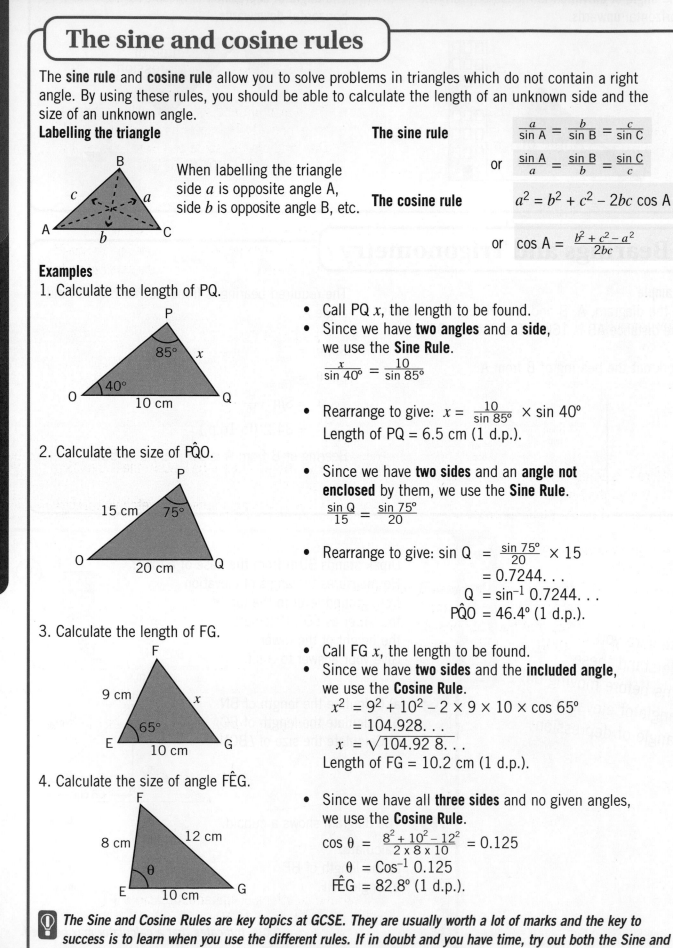

When labelling the triangle side a is opposite angle A, side b is opposite angle B, etc.

The sine rule

$$\frac{a}{\sin A} = \frac{b}{\sin B} = \frac{c}{\sin C}$$

or $\quad \frac{\sin A}{a} = \frac{\sin B}{b} = \frac{\sin C}{c}$

The cosine rule $\quad a^2 = b^2 + c^2 - 2bc \cos A$

or $\quad \cos A = \frac{b^2 + c^2 - a^2}{2bc}$

Examples

1. Calculate the length of PQ.

- Call PQ x, the length to be found.
- Since we have **two angles** and a **side**, we use the **Sine Rule**.
  $$\frac{x}{\sin 40°} = \frac{10}{\sin 85°}$$

- Rearrange to give: $x = \frac{10}{\sin 85°} \times \sin 40°$
  Length of PQ = 6.5 cm (1 d.p.).

2. Calculate the size of PQ̂O.

- Since we have **two sides** and an **angle not enclosed** by them, we use the **Sine Rule**.
  $$\frac{\sin Q}{15} = \frac{\sin 75°}{20}$$

- Rearrange to give: sin Q $= \frac{\sin 75°}{20} \times 15$
  $= 0.7244...$
  Q $= \sin^{-1} 0.7244...$
  PQ̂O $= 46.4°$ (1 d.p.).

3. Calculate the length of FG.

- Call FG x, the length to be found.
- Since we have **two sides** and the **included angle**, we use the **Cosine Rule**.
  $$x^2 = 9^2 + 10^2 - 2 \times 9 \times 10 \times \cos 65°$$
  $$= 104.928...$$
  $$x = \sqrt{104.928...}$$
  Length of FG = 10.2 cm (1 d.p.).

4. Calculate the size of angle FÊG.

- Since we have all **three sides** and no given angles, we use the **Cosine Rule**.
  $$\cos \theta = \frac{8^2 + 10^2 - 12^2}{2 \times 8 \times 10} = 0.125$$
  $$\theta = \text{Cos}^{-1} 0.125$$
  $$\text{FÊG} = 82.8° \text{ (1 d.p.).}$$

💡 *The Sine and Cosine Rules are key topics at GCSE. They are usually worth a lot of marks and the key to success is to learn when you use the different rules. If in doubt and you have time, try out both the Sine and Cosine Rules on your triangle; you should find that one of them won't work.*

Graphs of trigonometric functions

The behaviour of the sine, cosine and tangent functions may be represented graphically as shown below.

1) $y = \sin x$

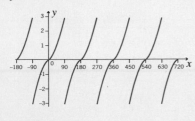

The maximum and minimum values of sin x are 1 and –1. The pattern repeats every 360°.

2) $y = \cos x$

The maximum and minimum values of cos x are 1 and –1. The pattern repeats every 360°. This graph is the same as $y = \sin x$ except it has been moved 90° to the left.

3) $y = \tan x$

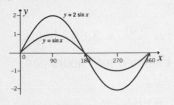

This graph is nothing like the two above. The values of tan x repeat every 180°. The tan of 90° is infinity, i.e. a value so great it cannot be written down.

> **Practise drawing the trigonometric graphs. You could be asked to sketch them in the exam.**

Other examples

1) $y = a \sin x$

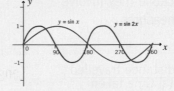

Here the points are stretched outwards in the y direction if $a > 1$.
If $a < 1$, they are pushed inwards.

2) $y = \sin (bx)$

Here the points are pushed in the x direction if $b < 1$.
If $b > 1$, all the points are stretched outwards.

The trigonometric graphs can be used to solve inverse problems.

Example

Solve sin x = 0.5 for values of x between 0 and 360°.
Draw a straight line across at y = 0.5 and by its symmetrical properties we can see that the solutions are:
x = 30° and 150°. (390° is out of the range.)

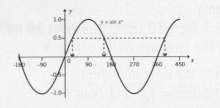

QUICK TEST

1 Calculate the missing length or angle marked x in these triangles.

a) 8 cm, 42°, 12 cm, x

b) 11 cm, 9 cm, x, 17 cm

c) x, 80 m, 70°, 40 m

d) 125°, 70°, x, 60 m

2 Find all the solutions of the equation $\sin x = \frac{2}{3}$ in the range $0° < x < 360°$.

Measures and measurement

Metric and imperial units

Metric units

Length	Weight	Capacity
10 mm = 1 cm	1000 mg = 1 g	1000 ml = 1 litre
100 cm = 1 m	1000 g = 1 kg	100 cl = 1 litre
1000 m = 1 km	1000 kg = 1 tonne	1000 cm³ = 1 litre

Imperial units

Length	Weight	Capacity
1 foot = 12 inches	1 stone = 14 pounds (lb)	20 fluid oz = 1 pint
1 yard = 3 feet	1 pound = 16 ounces (oz)	8 pints = 1 gallon

Compound measures

Speed can be measured in kilometres per hour (km/h), miles per hour (m.p.h.) and metres per second (m/s). km/h, m.p.h. and m/s are all **compound measures** because they involve a combination of basic measures.

Speed

$$\text{average speed} = \frac{\text{total distance travelled}}{\text{total time taken}}$$

$$s = \frac{d}{t}$$

Always check the units first, before starting a question. Change them if necessary.

Example
A car travels 50 miles in 1 hour 20 minutes. Find the speed in miles per hour.

Change the time units first:
20 minutes = $\frac{20}{60}$ of 1 hour

$$s = \frac{d}{t} = \frac{50}{1\frac{20}{60}} = 37.5 \text{ m.p.h.}$$

From the speed formula, two other formulae can be found.

$$\text{time} = \frac{\text{distance}}{\text{speed}} \quad \text{distance} = \text{speed} \times \text{time}$$

$$s = \frac{d}{t} \quad t = \frac{d}{s} \quad d = st$$

Just remember the letters.

Example
A car travels a distance of 240 miles at an average speed of 65 m.p.h.
How long does it take?

$$\text{time} = \frac{\text{distance}}{\text{speed}}, \text{ so } t = \frac{240}{65} = 3.692 \text{ hours}$$

3.692 hours must be changed into hours and minutes.

- Subtract the hours: 3.692 – 3 = 0.692
- Multiply the decimal part by 60 minutes. 0.692 × 60 = 42 minutes (nearest minute)
- Time taken = 3 hours 42 minutes

Density

$$\text{density} = \frac{\text{mass}}{\text{volume}} \quad \text{volume} = \frac{\text{mass}}{\text{density}}$$

$$\text{mass} = \text{density} \times \text{volume}$$

$$D = \frac{M}{V} \quad V = \frac{M}{D} \quad M = DV$$

Example
Find the density of an object whose mass is 400 g and whose volume is 25 cm³.

$$\text{density} = \frac{M}{V} = \frac{400}{25} = 16 \text{ g/cm}^3$$

Since the mass is in grams and volume is in cm³, density is in g/cm³.

Comparisons between metric and imperial units

Length	Weight	Capacity
2.5 cm ≈ 1 inch	25 g ≈ 1 ounce	1 litre ≈ $1\frac{3}{4}$ pints
30 cm ≈ 1 foot	1 kg ≈ 2.2 pounds	4.5 litres ≈ 1 gallon
1 m ≈ 39 inches		
8 km ≈ 5 miles		

Comparisons between metric and imperial units
are only approximate.

Example

Change 25 km into miles.

8 km ≈ 5 miles

1 km ≈ $\frac{5}{8}$ mile = 0.625 miles

25 km ≈ 25 × 0.625

= 15.625 miles

There is a lot of learning to do in this section. Try to learn all the metric and imperial conversions, and the formulae for speed, distance and time.

Accuracy of measurement

There are two types of measurements: discrete measurements and continuous measurements.

- **Discrete measures** are quantities that can be counted; for example, the number of baked bean tins on a shelf.
- **Continuous measures** are measurements which have been made by using a measuring instrument; for example, the height of a person. Continuous measures are not exact.

Example

Nigel weighs 72 kg to the nearest kg. His actual weight could be anywhere between 71.5 kg and 72.5 kg.

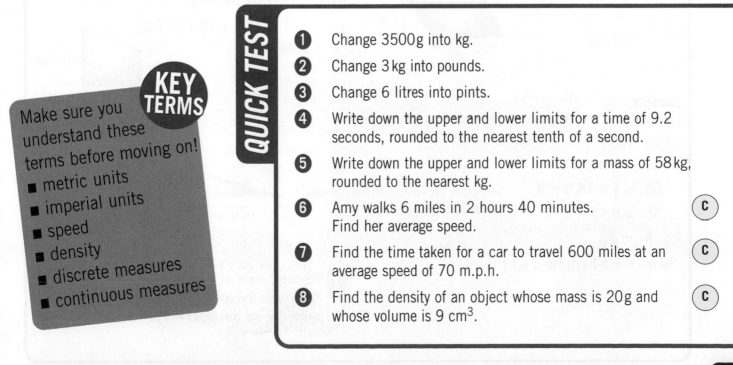

If W represents weight, then:

$$71.5 \leq W < 72.5$$

This is the **lower limit** of Nigel's weight (sometimes known as the **lower bound**). Anything below 71.5 would be recorded as 71 kg.

This is the **upper limit** (**upper bound**) of Nigel's weight. Anything from 72.5 upwards would be recorded as 73 kg.

KEY TERMS

Make sure you understand these terms before moving on!
- metric units
- imperial units
- speed
- density
- discrete measures
- continuous measures

QUICK TEST

1. Change 3500g into kg.

2. Change 3 kg into pounds.

3. Change 6 litres into pints.

4. Write down the upper and lower limits for a time of 9.2 seconds, rounded to the nearest tenth of a second.

5. Write down the upper and lower limits for a mass of 58 kg, rounded to the nearest kg.

6. Amy walks 6 miles in 2 hours 40 minutes. Find her average speed. **C**

7. Find the time taken for a car to travel 600 miles at an average speed of 70 m.p.h. **C**

8. Find the density of an object whose mass is 20g and whose volume is 9 cm³. **C**

Area of 2D shapes

Perimeter and area of 2D shapes

Perimeter: the distance around the outside edge of a shape.
Area: the amount of space a 2D shape covers.
Common units of area are square millimetres (mm²), square centimetres (cm²), square metres (m²), etc.

Areas of quadrilaterals and triangles

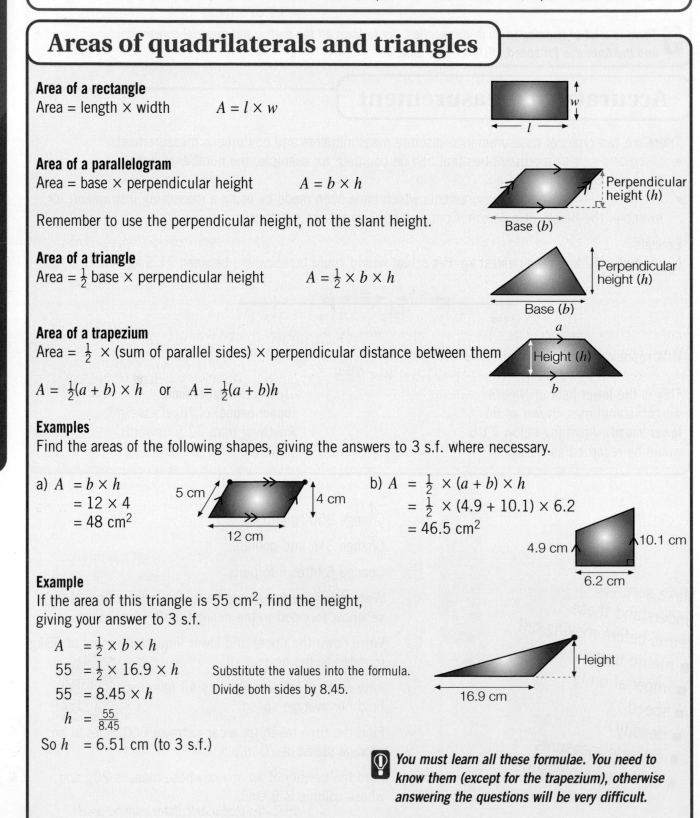

Area of a rectangle
Area = length × width $A = l \times w$

Area of a parallelogram
Area = base × perpendicular height $A = b \times h$

Remember to use the perpendicular height, not the slant height.

Area of a triangle
Area = ½ base × perpendicular height $A = \frac{1}{2} \times b \times h$

Area of a trapezium
Area = ½ × (sum of parallel sides) × perpendicular distance between them

$A = \frac{1}{2}(a + b) \times h$ or $A = \frac{1}{2}(a + b)h$

Examples
Find the areas of the following shapes, giving the answers to 3 s.f. where necessary.

a) $A = b \times h$
   $= 12 \times 4$
   $= 48 \text{ cm}^2$

5 cm   4 cm   12 cm

b) $A = \frac{1}{2} \times (a + b) \times h$
   $= \frac{1}{2} \times (4.9 + 10.1) \times 6.2$
   $= 46.5 \text{ cm}^2$

4.9 cm   10.1 cm   6.2 cm

Example
If the area of this triangle is 55 cm², find the height,
giving your answer to 3 s.f.

$A = \frac{1}{2} \times b \times h$
$55 = \frac{1}{2} \times 16.9 \times h$ Substitute the values into the formula.
$55 = 8.45 \times h$ Divide both sides by 8.45.
$h = \frac{55}{8.45}$
So $h = 6.51$ cm (to 3 s.f.)

Height   16.9 cm

You must learn all these formulae. You need to know them (except for the trapezium), otherwise answering the questions will be very difficult.

Changing area units

Example
The square has a length of 1 metre.
This is the same as a length of 100 cm.

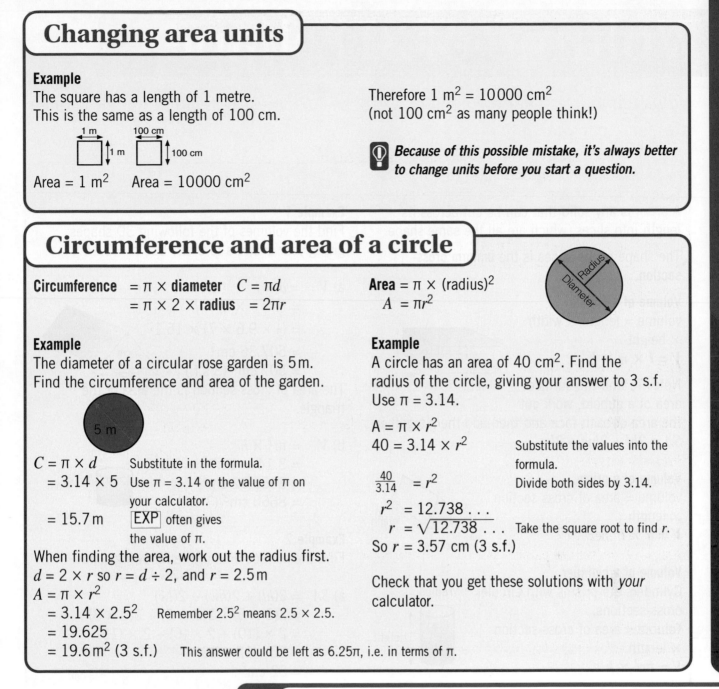

Area = 1 m²   Area = 10000 cm²

Therefore 1 m² = 10 000 cm²
(not 100 cm² as many people think!)

Because of this possible mistake, it's always better to change units before you start a question.

Circumference and area of a circle

Circumference = π × **diameter** $C = \pi d$
              = π × 2 × **radius** $= 2\pi r$

Area = π × (**radius**)² $A = \pi r^2$

Example
The diameter of a circular rose garden is 5 m.
Find the circumference and area of the garden.

5 m

$C = \pi \times d$ Substitute in the formula.
    = 3.14 × 5   Use π = 3.14 or the value of π on your calculator.
    = 15.7 m   EXP often gives the value of π.
When finding the area, work out the radius first.
$d = 2 \times r$ so $r = d \div 2$, and $r = 2.5$ m
$A = \pi \times r^2$
    = 3.14 × 2.5²   Remember 2.5² means 2.5 × 2.5.
    = 19.625
    = 19.6 m² (3 s.f.)   This answer could be left as 6.25π, i.e. in terms of π.

Example
A circle has an area of 40 cm². Find the radius of the circle, giving your answer to 3 s.f. Use π = 3.14.

$A = \pi \times r^2$
$40 = 3.14 \times r^2$ Substitute the values into the formula.
$\frac{40}{3.14} = r^2$ Divide both sides by 3.14.
$r^2 = 12.738 \ldots$
$r = \sqrt{12.738 \ldots}$ Take the square root to find r.
So $r = 3.57$ cm (3 s.f.)

Check that you get these solutions with *your* calculator.

KEY TERMS
Make sure you understand these terms before moving on!
- perimeter
- area
- circumference
- diameter
- radius

QUICK TEST

Work out the areas of the following shapes, giving your answers to 3 s.f.

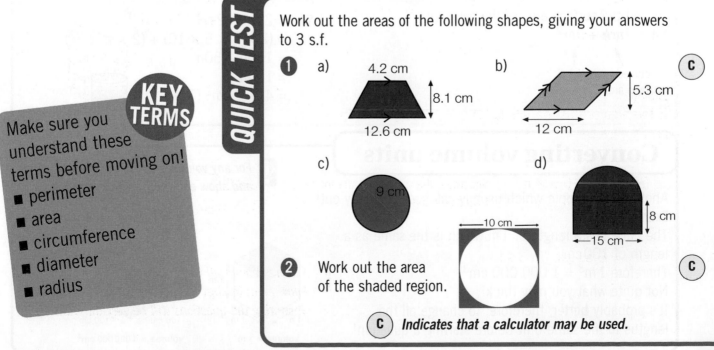

1. a) 4.2 cm   8.1 cm   12.6 cm
   b) 5.3 cm   12 cm   **C**
   c) 9 cm
   d) 8 cm   15 cm   **C**

2. Work out the area of the shaded region.   10 cm

C Indicates that a calculator may be used.

Volume of 3D shapes

Volume is the amount of space a 3D shape occupies. Common units of volume are mm³, cm³, m³, etc.

Volume of prisms

A **prism** is any solid that can be cut across its length into slices, which are all the same shape.

The shape of the slices is the **uniform cross-section**.

Volume of a cuboid
volume = length × width × height
$V = l \times w \times h$

Note: To find the surface area of a cuboid, work out the area of each face and then add them together
$SA = 2hl + 2hw + 2lw$

Volume of a prism
volume = area of cross-section × length
$V = a \times l$

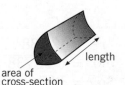

Volume of a cylinder
Cylinders are prisms with circular cross-sections.
volume = area of cross-section × length
$V = \pi r^2 \times h$

To find the surface area of the cylinder:
$SA = 2\pi rh + 2\pi r^2$
curved surface area — the 2 circles

Example 1
Find the volumes of the following 3D shapes, giving your answers to 3 s.f. Use π = 3.14.

a) $V = a \times l$
$= (\frac{1}{2} \times b \times h) \times l$
$= (\frac{1}{2} \times 9.6 \times 7) \times 15.1$
$= 507.36$ cm³
$= 507$ cm³ (3 s.f.)
The area of cross-section is the area of the triangle.

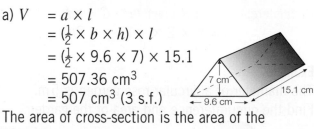

b) $V = \pi r^2 \times h$
$= 3.14 \times 10.7^2 \times 24.1$
$= 8663.92$ cm³
$= 8660$ cm³ (3 s.f.)

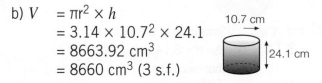

Example 2
Find the surface area of the following solids.

a) $SA = 2(hl) + 2(hw) + 2(lw)$
$= 2(2 \times 5) + 2(2 \times 3) + 2(5 \times 3)$
$= 2 \times (10) + 2 \times (6) + 2 \times (15)$
$= 20 + 12 + 30$
$= 62$ cm²

b) $SA = 2\pi rh + 2\pi r^2$
$= (2 \times \pi \times 5 \times 10) + (2 \times \pi \times 5^2)$
$= 100\pi + 50\pi$
$= 150\pi$
$= 471.2$ cm² (1 d.p.)

Converting volume units

Another tricky topic which usually catches everybody out!
Example
The cube has a length of 1 m which is the same as a length of 100 cm.
Therefore 1 m³ = 1 000 000 cm³
Not quite what you may think!
It's probably better, therefore, to change all the lengths to the same unit before starting a question!

> For any volume question work carefully and show each step in your working.

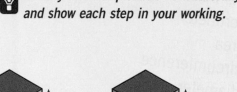

volume = 1 m³   volume = 1 000 000 cm³

Dimensions

- The **dimension** of **perimeter** is **length** (L); it is a measurement in one dimension.
- The dimension of **area** is **length × length** ($L \times L = L^2$); it is a measurement in two dimensions.
- The dimension of **volume** is **length × length × length** ($L \times L \times L = L^3$); it is a measurement in three dimensions.
- Values such as 3, $\frac{4}{\pi}$, 6.2 have no dimensions.
- The dimension of a formula cannot be greater than 3.

Examples
The letters a, b, c and d all represent lengths. For each expression, write down whether it represents a length, area or volume.

a) $a^2 + b^2$ = (length × length) + (length × length) = area $\qquad$ $L^2 + L^2$

b) $\frac{1}{3}\pi abc$ = number × length × length × length = volume $\qquad$ L^3

c) $2\pi a + \frac{3}{4}\pi d$ = (number × length) + (number × length) = length $\qquad$ $L + L$

d) $\frac{5}{9}\pi a^2 d + \pi b^2 c^2$ = (number × length × length × length) + (number × length^2 × length^2) = none

$\qquad\qquad\qquad\qquad\qquad\qquad\qquad\qquad\qquad$ $L^3 + L^4$ A dimension greater than 3 is impossible.

GCSE sample question

Here are some expressions.

$4\pi r^2$	$\frac{4}{5}pq^2$	$\sqrt{p^2 + q^2}$	$\pi p^2 q$	$\frac{5}{6}(pqr)$
✓	Volume	Length	Volume	Volume

$q(\sqrt{p^2 + r^2})$	$5q^2 r$	$\frac{\pi p^2 r}{q}$	$\frac{4\pi r^3}{pq}$
✓	Volume	✓	Length

The letters p, q and r represent length.
π, 4, 5 and 6 are numbers that have no dimensions.
Three of the expressions represent area.
Tick (✓) the boxes underneath these three expressions.
The red ticks indicate the answer to this question.

QUICK TEST

1. Work out the volumes of the following 3D shapes. Give your answers to 3 s.f.   a) [diagram: 6.5 cm, 19.8 cm, 27.2 cm]   b) [diagram: 85 cm, 10.6 cm]   **C**

2. The volume of a cylinder is 2000 cm^3 and its radius is 5.6 cm. Work out the height to 3 s.f.   **C**

3. x, y, z represent lengths. For each expression write down whether it could represent perimeter, area or volume.

   a) $\sqrt{x^2} + \sqrt{y^2} + \sqrt{z^2}$ b) $\frac{5}{9}\pi x^3 + 2y^3$

   c) $\frac{xyz^2}{3y}$ d) $\frac{9}{5}\pi xy + \frac{4}{5}\pi yz$

   C *Indicates that a calculator may be used.*

Further length, area and volume

On the higher tier paper you are required to find areas and volumes of more complex shapes and solids. Some of the formulae you will be given but the others you will need to learn.

Arc length, sector area and area of a segment

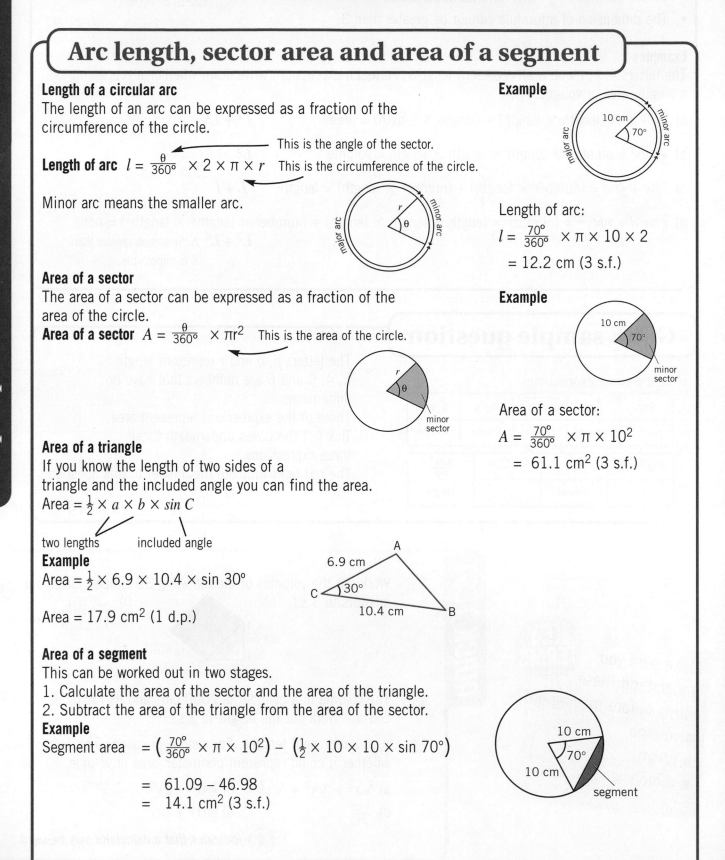

Length of a circular arc

The length of an arc can be expressed as a fraction of the circumference of the circle.

This is the angle of the sector.

Length of arc $l = \frac{\theta}{360°} \times 2 \times \pi \times r$ This is the circumference of the circle.

Minor arc means the smaller arc.

Example

Length of arc:

$l = \frac{70°}{360°} \times \pi \times 10 \times 2$

$= 12.2$ cm (3 s.f.)

Area of a sector

The area of a sector can be expressed as a fraction of the area of the circle.

Area of a sector $A = \frac{\theta}{360°} \times \pi r^2$ This is the area of the circle.

Example

Area of a sector:

$A = \frac{70°}{360°} \times \pi \times 10^2$

$= 61.1$ cm^2 (3 s.f.)

Area of a triangle

If you know the length of two sides of a triangle and the included angle you can find the area.

Area $= \frac{1}{2} \times a \times b \times sin\ C$

two lengths   included angle

Example

Area $= \frac{1}{2} \times 6.9 \times 10.4 \times sin\ 30°$

Area $= 17.9$ cm^2 (1 d.p.)

Area of a segment

This can be worked out in two stages.
1. Calculate the area of the sector and the area of the triangle.
2. Subtract the area of the triangle from the area of the sector.

Example

Segment area $= \left(\frac{70°}{360°} \times \pi \times 10^2 \right) - \left(\frac{1}{2} \times 10 \times 10 \times sin\ 70° \right)$

$= 61.09 - 46.98$

$= 14.1$ cm^2 (3 s.f.)

Spheres, pyramids and cones

Sphere

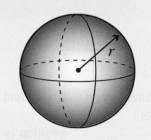

Volume of a sphere = $\frac{4}{3}\pi r^3$

Surface area of a sphere = $4\pi r^2$

> 💡 On the non-calculator paper you may be asked to find the volume of a solid. Don't be put off if it says leave your answer in terms of π; that just means leave the π in your calculation instead of working it out. Always show full working and learn the formulae.

Example
Find the volume and surface area of a sphere of radius = 10 cm.

Volume
$V = \frac{4}{3} \times \pi \times r^3$
$V = \frac{4}{3} \times \pi \times 10^3$
$= \frac{4000}{3} \times \pi$ cm^3
$= 4190$ cm^3 (3 s.f.)

Surface area SA $= 4 \times \pi \times r^2$
$= 4 \times \pi \times 10^2$
$= 400\pi$ cm^2
$= 1260$ cm^2 (3 s.f.)

- On the non-calculator paper you may be asked to leave your answer in terms of π.

Pyramids and cones
A cone is simply a pyramid with a circular base.

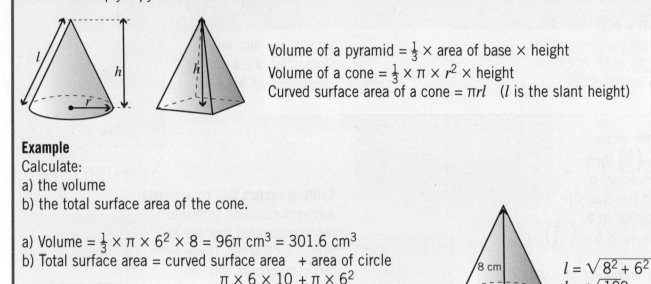

Volume of a pyramid = $\frac{1}{3}$ × area of base × height
Volume of a cone = $\frac{1}{3} \times \pi \times r^2$ × height
Curved surface area of a cone = πrl (l is the slant height)

Example
Calculate:
a) the volume
b) the total surface area of the cone.

a) Volume = $\frac{1}{3} \times \pi \times 6^2 \times 8 = 96\pi$ cm^3 = 301.6 cm^3
b) Total surface area = curved surface area   + area of circle
$\pi \times 6 \times 10 + \pi \times 6^2$
$60\pi + 36\pi$
Total surface area = 96π = 301.6 cm^2

$l = \sqrt{8^2 + 6^2}$
$l = \sqrt{100}$
$l = 10$ cm

8 cm   6 cm

KEY TERMS

Make sure you understand these terms before moving on!
- arc length
- sector area
- segment

QUICK TEST

❶ Calculate the arc length and sector area of AOB.

20 cm A
O 40°
B

❷ Calculate the total volume of this solid, leaving your answer in terms of π.

6 cm
5 cm   10 cm

Ⓒ Indicates that a calculator may be used.

Ⓒ

Ⓒ

Shape, space and measures

Vectors

Important points

Vectors have both size or **magnitude** and **direction**. Four types of notation are used to represent vectors.
The vector shown here can be referred to as:

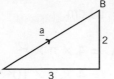

$\binom{3}{2}$ or **a** or <u>a</u> or $\overrightarrow{AB}$

The direction of the vector is shown on the diagram by using an arrow.

If two vectors are equal then they are parallel and equal in length.

If $\overrightarrow{AB} = k\overrightarrow{CD}$ then $\overrightarrow{AB}$ and $\overrightarrow{CD}$ are parallel and the length of $\overrightarrow{AB}$ is k times the length of $\overrightarrow{CD}$.

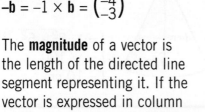

$\overrightarrow{CD} = 2\overrightarrow{AB}$

If the vector
$\mathbf{b} = \binom{4}{3}$ then
the vector **−b**
is in the opposite
direction to **b**.
$-\mathbf{b} = -1 \times \mathbf{b} = \binom{-4}{-3}$

The **magnitude** of a vector is the length of the directed line segment representing it. If the vector is expressed in column form, then Pythagoras' theorem can be used to find the magnitude.

In general the magnitude of a vector $\binom{x}{y}$ is
$\sqrt{x^2 + y^2}$

The magnitude of AB is given by:
$$(AB)^2 = 4^2 + 3^2$$
$$(AB)^2 = 16 + 9$$
$$(AB)^2 = 25$$
$$AB = \sqrt{25}$$
$$AB = 5$$
The magnitude of $\overrightarrow{AB}$ is 5 units.

Adding and subtracting vectors

The **resultant** of two vectors is found by **vector addition** or **subtraction**. Vectors must always be combined end to end so that the arrows follow on from each other. A resultant is usually labelled with a double arrow.

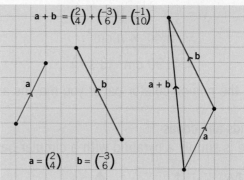

$\mathbf{a} + \mathbf{b} = \binom{2}{4} + \binom{-3}{6} = \binom{-1}{10}$

$\mathbf{a} = \binom{2}{4} \qquad \mathbf{b} = \binom{-3}{6}$

Vectors can also be subtracted. **a − b** can be interpreted as **a + (−b)**.

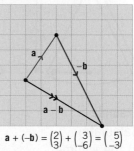

$\mathbf{a} + (-\mathbf{b}) = \binom{2}{3} + \binom{3}{-6} = \binom{5}{-3}$

Splitting vectors into components

Any vector can be split into two components that are at 90° to each other. These two components will be $F\cos\theta$ and $F\sin\theta$.

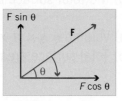

Position vectors

The position vector of a point P is the vector $\overrightarrow{OP}$ where O is the origin.

In the diagram, the position vectors of C and D are **c** and **d** respectively.

Using this notation:
1) $\overrightarrow{CD} = -\mathbf{c} + \mathbf{d}$ or
   $\overrightarrow{CD} = \mathbf{d} - \mathbf{c}$

2) $\overrightarrow{OM} = \mathbf{c} + \frac{1}{2}(\mathbf{d} - \mathbf{c})$
   $= \frac{1}{2}(\mathbf{d} + \mathbf{c})$
   where M is the midpoint of CD.

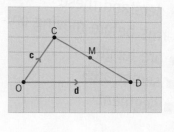

Typical GCSE questions

Example 1

Given that $\vec{OA}$ = **a**
$\vec{OB}$ = **b**, $\vec{OC}$ = **c**
and that N splits $\vec{AB}$
in the ratio 1 : 2, find
the following vectors.

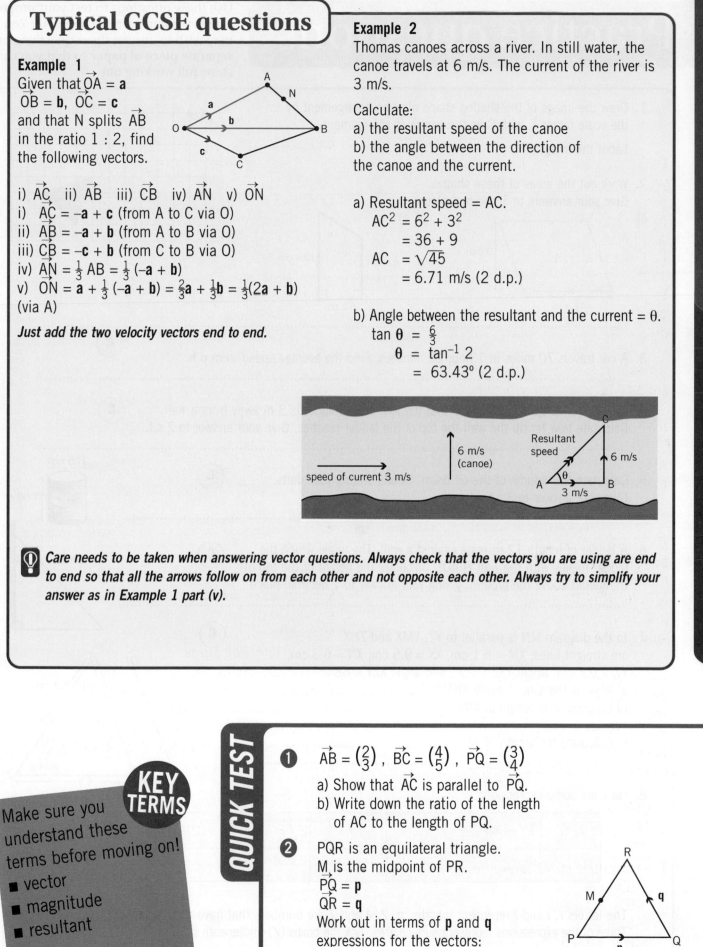

i) $\vec{AC}$ ii) $\vec{AB}$ iii) $\vec{CB}$ iv) $\vec{AN}$ v) $\vec{ON}$

i) $\vec{AC}$ = –**a** + **c** (from A to C via O)
ii) $\vec{AB}$ = –**a** + **b** (from A to B via O)
iii) $\vec{CB}$ = –**c** + **b** (from C to B via O)
iv) $\vec{AN}$ = $\frac{1}{3}$ AB = $\frac{1}{3}$ (–**a** + **b**)
v) $\vec{ON}$ = **a** + $\frac{1}{3}$ (–**a** + **b**) = $\frac{2}{3}$**a** + $\frac{1}{3}$**b** = $\frac{1}{3}$(2**a** + **b**)
(via A)

Just add the two velocity vectors end to end.

Example 2

Thomas canoes across a river. In still water, the canoe travels at 6 m/s. The current of the river is 3 m/s.

Calculate:
a) the resultant speed of the canoe
b) the angle between the direction of the canoe and the current.

a) Resultant speed = AC.
$AC^2 = 6^2 + 3^2$
$= 36 + 9$
$AC = \sqrt{45}$
$= 6.71$ m/s (2 d.p.)

b) Angle between the resultant and the current = θ.
$\tan θ = \frac{6}{3}$
$θ = \tan^{-1} 2$
$= 63.43°$ (2 d.p.)

speed of current 3 m/s

6 m/s (canoe)

Resultant speed

6 m/s

3 m/s

> Care needs to be taken when answering vector questions. Always check that the vectors you are using are end to end so that all the arrows follow on from each other and not opposite each other. Always try to simplify your answer as in Example 1 part (v).

KEY TERMS

Make sure you understand these terms before moving on!

- vector
- magnitude
- resultant

QUICK TEST

1 $\vec{AB} = \binom{2}{3}$, $\vec{BC} = \binom{4}{5}$, $\vec{PQ} = \binom{3}{4}$

a) Show that $\vec{AC}$ is parallel to $\vec{PQ}$.
b) Write down the ratio of the length of AC to the length of PQ.

2 PQR is an equilateral triangle.
M is the midpoint of PR.
$\vec{PQ}$ = **p**
$\vec{QR}$ = **q**
Work out in terms of **p** and **q** expressions for the vectors:

a) $\vec{PR}$ b) $\vec{MQ}$

Practice questions

Use these questions to test your progress. Check your answers on page 110. You may wish to answer these questions on a separate piece of paper so that you can show full working out.

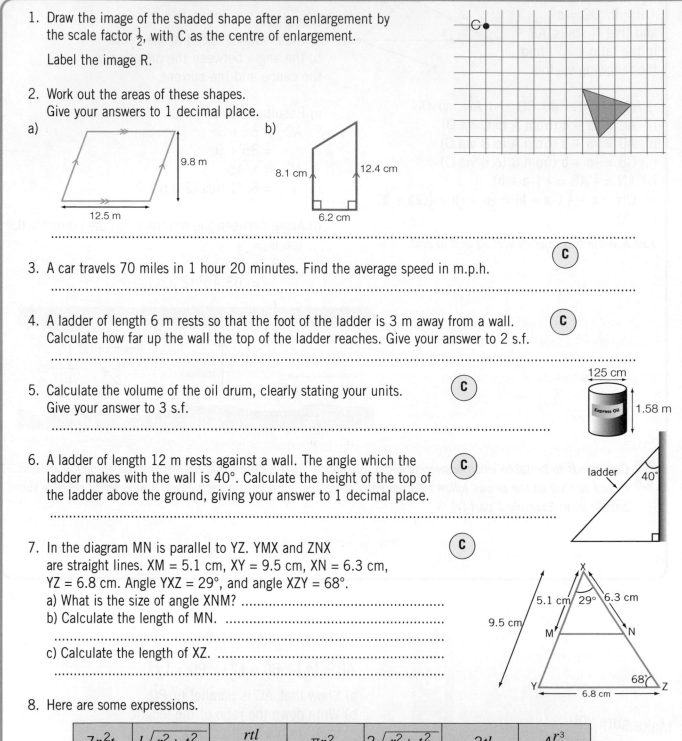

1. Draw the image of the shaded shape after an enlargement by the scale factor $\frac{1}{2}$, with C as the centre of enlargement.

   Label the image R.

2. Work out the areas of these shapes.
   Give your answers to 1 decimal place.

   a)

   9.8 m

   12.5 m

   b)

   8.1 cm   12.4 cm

   6.2 cm

   ....

3. A car travels 70 miles in 1 hour 20 minutes. Find the average speed in m.p.h. **C**

   ....

4. A ladder of length 6 m rests so that the foot of the ladder is 3 m away from a wall. **C**
   Calculate how far up the wall the top of the ladder reaches. Give your answer to 2 s.f.

   ....

5. Calculate the volume of the oil drum, clearly stating your units. **C**
   Give your answer to 3 s.f.

   125 cm

   Express Oil   1.58 m

   ....

6. A ladder of length 12 m rests against a wall. The angle which the **C**
   ladder makes with the wall is 40°. Calculate the height of the top of
   the ladder above the ground, giving your answer to 1 decimal place.

   ladder   40°

   ....

7. In the diagram MN is parallel to YZ. YMX and ZNX **C**
   are straight lines. XM = 5.1 cm, XY = 9.5 cm, XN = 6.3 cm,
   YZ = 6.8 cm. Angle YXZ = 29°, and angle XZY = 68°.
   a) What is the size of angle XNM? ....
   b) Calculate the length of MN. ....

   ....

   c) Calculate the length of XZ. ....

   ....

   X
   5.1 cm 29° 6.3 cm
   9.5 cm M   N
   Y   6.8 cm   68° Z

8. Here are some expressions.

$7r^2t$	$l\sqrt{r^2+t^2}$	$\dfrac{rtl}{4}$	πr^2	$2\sqrt{r^2+t^2}$	$2tl$	$4\dfrac{r^3}{t^2}$

   The letters r, t and l represent lengths. π, 2, 4 and 7 are numbers that have no dimensions.
   Three of the expressions represent surface area. Tick the boxes (✓) underneath these three expressions.

C *Indicates that a calculator may be used.*

9. Find the arc length and area of the sector. (C)

....

10. Find the volume of this metal container. (C)

....

11. The volume of this cone is 500 cm³. (C)
Calculate the length of the radius.

....

12. The surface area of a cone is 120 cm². What is the surface area of a similar cone which is four times as high? (C)

....

13. The two spheres are similar. If the volume of the larger sphere is (C)
2145 cm³ to 4 s.f., calculate the volume of the smaller sphere.

....

14. The diagram shows a triangle RST. B is the midpoint of RT and A is the point on
RS such that AS = 2RA. $\overrightarrow{RA}$ = **r** and $\overrightarrow{RB}$ = **t**.
a) Write $\overrightarrow{AB}$ in terms of **r** and **t**.

....

b) Write $\overrightarrow{AT}$ in terms of **r** and **t**.

....

c) Write down $\overrightarrow{ST}$ in terms of **r** and **t**.

....

15. Work out all the solutions of 2cos$x$ = 1 for values of x in the range −360° ≤ x ≤ 360°. (C)

....

16. Work out the size of the lettered side or angle in each triangle. (C)

(a)

(b)

(c)

(d)

....

....

....

17. In the diagram AB represents a vertical tower on level ground. R and S are two
points due west of B. The distance RS is 50 m. The angles of elevation of A from (C)
S and R are 40° and 60° respectively.
Calculate the height in metres of the tower, AB.

....

18. Find the size of each of the lettered angles.

....

(a)   (b)   (c)   (d)

How well did you do?   ✗ 0–5 Try again   6–11 Getting there   12–14 Good work   15–18 Excellent! ✓

Collecting data

The census is one of the largest surveys that takes place. The census is done every 10 years and its main aim is to give a 'snapshot' of Britain at the time. In order to carry out the census all households are given a survey to complete.

Types of data

There are two main types of data:

Quantitative
The answer is a number, e.g. How many blue cars are there in a car park?

Qualitative
The answer is a word, e.g. What is your favourite colour?

Quantitative data can be discrete or continuous.

- **Discrete data** has an exact value. Each category is separate and is usually found by counting. Examples include the number of people with brown hair.

- **Continuous data** has values that merge from one category to the next. Examples include the heights and weights of students. Continuous data cannot be measured exactly. The accuracy of the measurement relies on the accuracy of the measuring equipment.

- **Primary data** is data that is collected by the person who is going to analyse and use it.

- **Secondary data** is data that is available from an external source, such as books, newspapers and the internet.

Hypotheses and experiments

A hypothesis is a **prediction** that can be tested.
Experiments can be used to test hypotheses.

Example

Hypothesis: The better the light, the faster seedlings grow.

Variable: This is the intensity of the light, which can be changed.

Conditions: The other conditions must stay the same. All seedlings must be exactly the same size, strength and colour to start with. If there is **bias** (e.g. if one side of the tray gets extra water), then the experiment needs to start again.

Two-way tables

Data can be collected and displayed in a two-way table.

Example
The table shows the results of a survey of the languages studied by students in a school.

The table is completed with the figures shown in red.

	French	Spanish	German	Total
Female	16	9	1	26
Male	12	12	8	32
Total	28	21	9	58

Questionnaires

These can be used to test hypotheses.

When designing questionnaires:

✓ Decide what you need to find out: the **hypothesis**.

✓ Give instructions on how the questionnaire has to be filled in.

✓ Do not ask for information that is not needed (e.g. name).

✓ Make the questions clear and concise.

✓ Keep the questionnaire short.

✓ If people's opinions are needed, make sure the question is **unbiased**.
An example of a biased question would be:
'Do you agree that a leisure centre should have a tennis court rather than a squash court?'

✓ Allow for all possible answers, for example:
'Which of these is your favourite colour?'

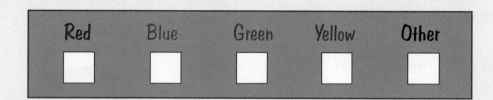

Red	Blue	Green	Yellow	Other
☐	☐	☐	☐	☐

💡 *When asked to design a questionnaire, always word the questions carefully.*
Try to avoid bias appearing in your questions.

Sampling

This is an efficient way of collecting information about a population. It is important that the sample is representative of the population and does not contain bias. The bigger the sample, the more accurate the results will be.

There are three main methods of sampling.

1. Random sampling
In a random sample each member of the population has an equal chance of being chosen.

2. Stratified sampling
Usually the population is divided into groups (**strata**) that have something in common, such as age. A simple random sample is then taken from each group. The same proportion of the group is used for each sample.

3. Selective sample
Every nth item is chosen and the value of n is selected at random.

KEY TERMS

Make sure you understand these terms before moving on!
- quantitative
- qualitative
- discrete
- continuous
- hypothesis
- stratified sampling

QUICK TEST

❶ Design a questionnaire you could give a friend in order to find out what they do in their spare time.

❷ Samuel is carrying out a survey on homework; he decides to use a stratified sample and ask 100 students. Calculate the number of students he will ask from each group.

	Frequency
Year 7	120
Year 8	150
Year 9	230

Representing data

Drawing pie charts

Pie charts are used to illustrate data. They are circles split up into sections, each section representing a certain category of the data or number of items.

Example
The table shows the favourite sports of 24 students in year 11.
Draw a pie chart to show this data.

Sport	Frequency
Football	9
Swimming	5
Netball	3
Hockey	7
Total	24

To calculate the angles for the pie chart:
- Find the total of the frequencies.
- Find the fraction of the total for each category.
- Multiply the fraction by 360° to find the angle.

Sport	Frequency	Angle	Workings
Football	9	135°	$\frac{9}{24} \times 360°$
Swimming	5	75°	$\frac{5}{24} \times 360°$
Netball	3	45°	$\frac{3}{24} \times 360°$
Hockey	7	105°	$\frac{7}{24} \times 360°$
Total	24	360°	

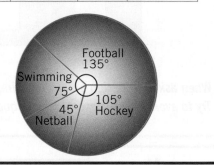

Interpreting pie charts

Example
The pie chart shows how 18 students travel to school.
How many travel by a) car, b) bus and c) foot?
360° = 18 students
$1° = \frac{18}{360} = 0.05$ (Work out what 1° represents.)
a) Car: 60° × 0.05 = 3 students
b) Bus: 80° × 0.05 = 4 students
c) Foot: 220° × 0.05 = 11 students

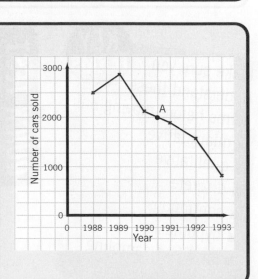

Pie chart questions are usually worth about 4 marks at GCSE. Make sure the angles add up to 360° before drawing it. Measure the angles carefully since you are allowed only a 2° tolerance.

Line graphs

- A **line graph** is a set of points joined by lines.

Year	1988	1989	1990	1991	1992	1993
Number of cars sold	2500	2900	2100	1900	1600	800

- **Middle values**, like point A, have no meaning.
  Point A does **not** show that halfway between 1990 and 1991 there were 2000 cars sold.

This example is known as a time series because the data is recorded at intervals of time.

Histograms

- Histograms illustrate **continuous data**. They are similar to bar charts except that there are no gaps between the bars. The data must be grouped into **equal** class intervals if the length of the bar is used to represent the frequency.

Example
The masses of 30 workers in a factory are shown in the table:

- $45 \leqslant W < 55$ is called a **class interval**. In this example the class intervals are all equal in width. $45 \leqslant W < 55$ means the masses are at least 45 but less than 55 kg. A mass of 55 kg would be in the next group.

Note:
- The axes do not need to start at zero.
- The axes are labelled.
- The graph has a title.

Mass (W kg)	Frequency
$45 \leqslant W < 55$	7
$55 \leqslant W < 65$	13
$65 \leqslant W < 75$	6
$75 \leqslant W < 85$	4

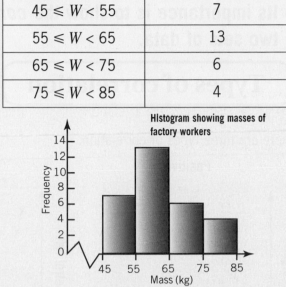

Histogram showing masses of factory workers

Frequency polygons

A **frequency polygon** joins the **midpoints** of the tops of the bars of **class intervals** for grouped or continuous data. Consider the histogram of the factory workers again.
- Put a cross at the middle of the top of each bar and join the crosses up with a ruler.
- Draw a line down from the middles of the first and last bar to the x-axis to form a closed polygon, OR
- To form an open polygon do not join to the x-axis.

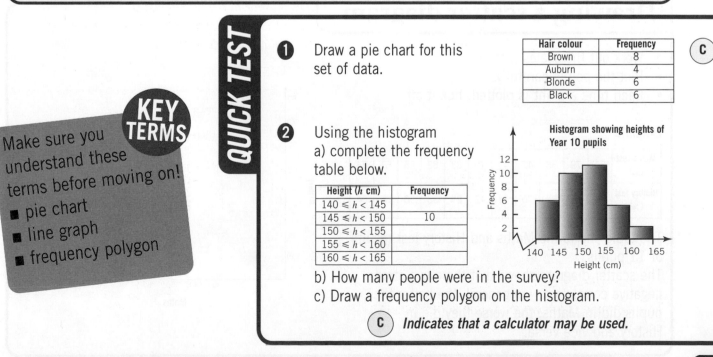

KEY TERMS

Make sure you understand these terms before moving on!
- pie chart
- line graph
- frequency polygon

QUICK TEST

1 Draw a pie chart for this set of data.

Hair colour	Frequency
Brown	8
Auburn	4
Blonde	6
Black	6

C

2 Using the histogram
a) complete the frequency table below.

Height (h cm)	Frequency
$140 \leqslant h < 145$	
$145 \leqslant h < 150$	10
$150 \leqslant h < 155$	
$155 \leqslant h < 160$	
$160 \leqslant h < 165$	

Histogram showing heights of Year 10 pupils

b) How many people were in the survey?
c) Draw a frequency polygon on the histogram.

C *Indicates that a calculator may be used.*

Scatter diagrams and correlation

- **A scatter diagram (scatter graph or scatter plot) is used to show two sets of data at the same time.**
- **Its importance is to show the *correlation* (connection) between two sets of data.**

Types of correlation

There are three types of correlation.

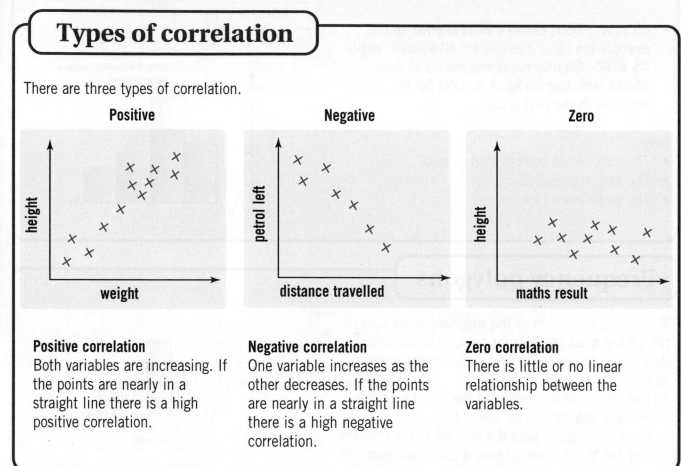

Positive

Negative

Zero

Positive correlation
Both variables are increasing. If the points are nearly in a straight line there is a high positive correlation.

Negative correlation
One variable increases as the other decreases. If the points are nearly in a straight line there is a high negative correlation.

Zero correlation
There is little or no linear relationship between the variables.

Drawing a scatter diagram

- Work out the scales first.
- Plot the points carefully.
- Each time a point is plotted, tick it off.

Example

Maths test (%)	64	79	38	42	49	75	83	82	66	61	54
History test (%)	70	36	84	70	74	42	29	33	50	56	64

The table shows the Maths and History test results of 11 pupils.
The scatter diagram shows that there is a strong negative correlation – in general, the better the pupils did in Maths, the worse they did in History and vice versa.

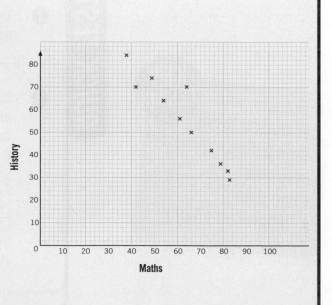

Lines of best fit

- This is **the line that best fits the data**. It goes in the direction of the data and there is roughly the same number of points above the line as below it.
- A **line of best fit** can be used to make predictions.

Example

If Hassam was away for a Maths test but got 78% in History then from the scatter diagram you can estimate he would have got approximately 43% in Maths.

Go to 78% on the History scale. Read across to the line then down.

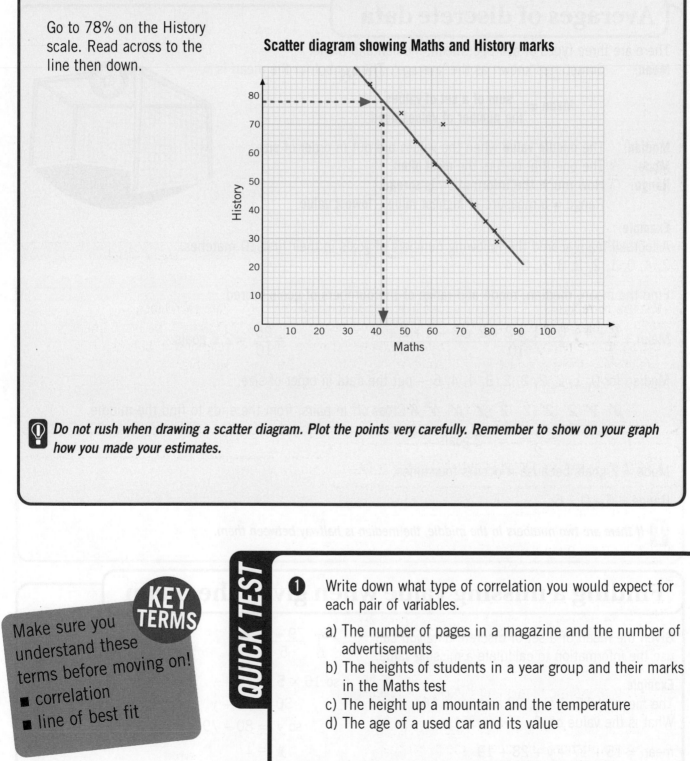

Scatter diagram showing Maths and History marks

💡 *Do not rush when drawing a scatter diagram. Plot the points very carefully. Remember to show on your graph how you made your estimates.*

QUICK TEST

① Write down what type of correlation you would expect for each pair of variables.

a) The number of pages in a magazine and the number of advertisements

b) The heights of students in a year group and their marks in the Maths test

c) The height up a mountain and the temperature

d) The age of a used car and its value

Averages 1

'Average height of students is 163 cm.'

Averages of discrete data

There are three types of average: mean, median and mode.

Mean: Sometimes known as the 'average'. The symbol for the mean is $\bar{x}$.

$$\text{Mean} = \frac{\text{sum of a set of values}}{\text{the number of values used}}$$

Median: The **middle value** when the values are put in order of size.

Mode: The one that occurs the **most often**.

Range: How much the information is **spread**.

            Range = a measure of **highest value – lowest value**.

Example

A football team scored the following numbers of goals in their first 10 matches.

2, 4, 0, 1, 2, 2, 3, 6, 2, 4

Find the mean, median, mode and range of the numbers of goals scored.

$$\text{Mean} = \frac{2 + 4 + 0 + 1 + 2 + 2 + 3 + 6 + 2 + 4}{10} \qquad = \frac{26}{10} = 2.6 \text{ goals}$$

Median for 0, 1, 2, 2, 2, 2, 3, 4, 4, 6 – put the data in order of size.

$\cancel{0} \;\; \cancel{1} \;\; \cancel{2} \;\; \cancel{2} \;\; \boxed{2 \quad 2} \;\; \cancel{3} \;\; \cancel{4} \;\; \cancel{4} \;\; \cancel{6}$ Cross off in pairs, from the ends to find the middle.

$$\frac{2 + 2}{2} = 2 \text{ goals}$$

Mode = 2 goals because it occurs four times.

Range = 6 – 0 = 6

> 💡 *If there are two numbers in the middle, the median is halfway between them.*

Finding a missing value when given the mean

Given the mean of a set of discrete data you can use the information to calculate a missing value.

Example

The mean of 15, 17, y, 28 and 19 is 16.
What is the value of y?

$$\text{mean} = \frac{15 + 17 + y + 28 + 19}{5}$$

$$16 = \frac{79 + y}{5}$$

so $16 \times 5 = 79 + y$ This is now a simple equation

$$80 = 79 + y \qquad \text{to solve.}$$

so $y = 80 - 79$

$$y = 1$$

The missing value is 1.

Finding averages from a frequency table

A frequency table tells you how many data items there are in a group.

Example

Number of sisters (x)	0	1	2	3	4
Frequency (f)	4	9	3	5	2

This means 2 people had 4 sisters.

If there are two numbers in the middle, the median is half way between them

Mean ($\bar{x}$) $= \dfrac{\Sigma fx}{\Sigma f}$ (Σ means the sum of)

$= \dfrac{(4 \times 0) + (9 \times 1) + (3 \times 2) + (5 \times 3) + (2 \times 4)}{4 + 9 + 3 + 5 + 2 + 0}$

$= \dfrac{38}{23} = 1.7$ (to 1 d.p.)

Median Since there are 23 people who have been asked, the median will be the 12th person in the table.

11 people	12	11 people

The 12th person has 1 sister ∴ the median = 1

Mode This is the data value with the highest frequency, that is 1 sister.

Range 4 − 0 = 4

 When finding the mean from a frequency table remember to divide by the sum of the frequencies and not by how many groups there are.

Moving averages

Moving averages are used to smooth out the changes in a set of data that varies over a period of time. A four-point moving average uses four data items in each calculation; a three-point moving average uses three and so on.

A moving average can often give a good idea of any trend in a set of data as well as enabling you to draw a trend line on a **time series graph**.

Example
Find a three-point moving average for the following data.
2, 4, 0, 1, 2, 2, 3, 6, 2, 4
Average for first three data points:
$(2 + 4 + 0) \div 3 = 2$
Average for data points $(4 + 0 + 1) \div 3 = 1.\dot{6}$
$(2 \rightarrow 4)$ and so on... $(0 + 1 + 2) \div 3 = 1$
$(1 + 2 + 2) \div 3 = 1.\dot{6}$
$(2 + 2 + 3) \div 3 = 2.\dot{3}$
$(2 + 3 + 6) \div 3 = 3.\dot{6}$
$(3 + 6 + 2) \div 3 = 3.\dot{6}$
$(6 + 2 + 4) \div 3 = 4$

KEY TERMS

Make sure you understand these terms before moving on!
- mean
- median
- mode
- range
- moving average

QUICK TEST

❶ Find the mean, median, mode and range of this set of data. **C**
2, 9, 3, 6, 4, 4, 5, 8, 4

❷ Charlotte made this table for the numbers of minutes students were late for registration. **C**

Number of minutes late (x)	0	1	2	3	4
Frequency (f)	10	4	6	3	2

Calculate:
a) the mean   b) the median   c) the mode   d) the range.

C *Indicates that a calculator may be used.*

Averages 2

Stem-and-leaf diagrams

Stem-and-leaf diagrams are used for recording and displaying information. They can also be used to find the mode, median and range of a set of data.

Example

These are marks gained by some students in a mathematics exam.

24	61	55	36	42
32	60	51	38	58
55	52	47	55	55

When the information is put into a stem-and-leaf diagram it looks like this:

```
stem | leaf
  2  | 4
  3  | 6 2 8
  4  | 2 7
  5  | 5 1 8 5 2 5 5
  6  | 1 0      Stem = 10 marks
```

It is more useful to put the 'leaves' in order, like this:

```
stem | leaf
  2  | 4
  3  | 2 6 8        Stem is 3, leaf is 2,
  4  | 2 7          value is 32.
  5  | 1 2 5 5 5 5 8
  6  | 0 1      Stem = 10 marks
```

To read off the values you multiply the stem by 10 and add on the leaf. Using the stem-and-leaf, the mode, median and range can be found easily.

mode	= 55
median	= 52
range	= 61 – 24 = 37

Stem-and-leaf diagrams are useful when comparing two sets of data.

Using appropriate averages

- The **mean** is useful when you need a 'typical' value.
  Be careful not to use the mean if there are extreme values.
- The **median** is a useful average if there are extreme values.
- The **mode** is useful when you need the most common value.

Using averages and spread to compare distributions

Be careful when drawing conclusions from averages as they do not always tell the whole story.

Example

  11A obtained a mean of 57% in a science test.
  11T obtained a mean of 84% in the same test.

From the averages you might say that 11T is better at science than 11A.

However if you look at the range for each class:

  11A = 100% – 21% = 79%
  11T = 94% – 76% = 18%

Using the range it can be seen that not all of 11T are better at science than 11A, because some of 11A obtained higher marks than 11T. The average of 11A has been lowered because of the low marks obtained by some pupils.

Averages of grouped data

- When the data values are grouped into class intervals, the exact data values are not known.
- You can estimate the mean by using the **midpoint** of the **class** interval.
- The midpoint is the halfway value.
- When you are using grouped (continuous) data you can only find the **modal class**. This is the one with the highest frequency.

Typical GCSE question

Finding the mean of grouped data is a very common GCSE question and is usually worth about 4 marks.

Example
The table shows the masses of some Year 9 pupils.

Mass (W kg)	Frequency (f)	Midpoint (x)	fx
$40 \leqslant W < 45$	7	42.5	297.5
$45 \leqslant W < 50$	4	47.5	190
$50 \leqslant W < 55$	3	52.5	157.5
$55 \leqslant W < 60$	1	57.5	57.5

Adding these extra columns helps to show your working out.

This is the same as on page 95 except that the frequency is multiplied by the **midpoint value**.

Mean
$$= \frac{\Sigma fx}{\Sigma f} = \frac{(7 \times 42.5) + (4 \times 47.5) + (3 \times 52.5) + (1 \times 57.5)}{7 + 4 + 3 + 1}$$
$$= \frac{702.5}{15} = 46.8 \text{ kg (1 d.p.)}$$

Modal class is $40 \leqslant W < 45$

> If your calculator will do statistical calculations, learn how to use it. It is much quicker but always do it twice as a check. Always try and show full working out in order to obtain some method marks.

KEY TERMS

Make sure you understand these terms before moving on!
- stem-and-leaf diagram
- modal class

QUICK TEST

❶ The heights of some Year 10 pupils are shown in the table. Ⓒ

Height (h cm)	Frequency
$140 \leqslant h < 145$	4
$145 \leqslant h < 150$	7
$150 \leqslant h < 155$	14
$155 \leqslant h < 160$	5
$160 \leqslant h < 165$	2

a) Calculate an estimate for the mean of this data.
b) Write down the modal class.

Ⓒ *Indicates that a calculator may be used.*

Cumulative frequency graphs

Cumulative frequency graphs are very useful for finding the median and the spread of grouped data.

Typical GCSE question

Ahmed carried out a survey for his Geography coursework. He recorded the distances that 200 people travelled to an out-of-town shopping centre. The table shows his findings.

Distance (*d* miles)	Frequency
$0 \leqslant d < 5$	12
$5 \leqslant d < 10$	49
$10 \leqslant d < 15$	57
$15 \leqslant d < 20$	45
$20 \leqslant d < 25$	34
$25 \leqslant d < 30$	3

Distance (*d* miles)	Cumulative frequency
$0 \leqslant d < 5$	12
$0 \leqslant d < 10$	61
$0 \leqslant d < 15$	118
$0 \leqslant d < 20$	163
$0 \leqslant d < 25$	197
$0 \leqslant d < 30$	200

- To complete the cumulative frequency table add the frequencies, e.g. 12 + 49 = 61.
- If the cumulative frequency table is correct, the final value in the cumulative frequency column should be the same as the number of people in the survey.
- Plot (5, 12), (10, 61), ... Note that the **upper class** boundaries are used.
- Since no people travelled a negative distance, the graph starts at (0, 0).
- Join the points with a smooth curve.

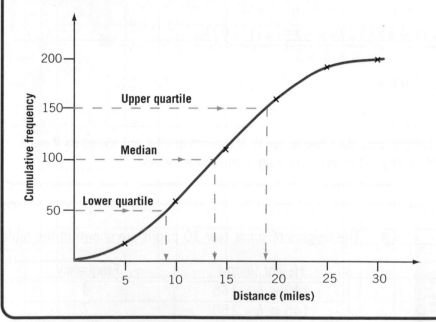

> **Cumulative frequency graphs are a common topic tested on the GCSE Higher level examination. Remember to:**
> - *Draw graphs as accurately as possible. Try to avoid bumpy curves.*
> - *Check your graph looks like an S shape.*
> - *Plot the upper class boundaries.*
> - *Show the method lines for the median, etc. on your graphs.*

Finding the median

The **median** is the middle value of the distribution.
For Ahmed's distance data:

median = $\frac{1}{2}$ × total cumulative frequency = $\frac{1}{2}$ × 200 = 100

- Reading across from 100 to the graph and then down gives a median distance of about 13.4 miles.

Finding the interquartile range

The **interquartile range** is found by subtracting the **lower quartile** (LQ) from the **upper quartile** (UQ).
- **Interquartile range** = upper quartile – lower quartile
- The **upper quartile** is the value three quarters of the way into the distribution.

   So $\frac{3}{4} \times 200 = 150$ which gives an approximate value of 18.7 miles for Ahmed's data.
- The **lower quartile** is the value one quarter of the way into the distribution.

   So $\frac{1}{4} \times 200 = 50$ which gives an approximate value of 9 miles for Ahmed's data.

   The interquartile range for Ahmed's data is 18.7 – 9 = 9.7 miles.

Using the interquartile range
A large interquartile range indicates that the 'middle half' of the data is widely spread about the median.
A small interquartile range indicates that the 'middle half' of the data is concentrated about the median.

Box-and-whisker diagrams

All cumulative frequency graphs tend to have the same basic shape so it is not easy to compare two or more sets of data.

A **box-and-whisker diagram** (or box plots) shows the interquartile range as a box, which makes it useful when comparing distributions.

The box-and-whisker diagram for the cumulative frequency graph of Ahmed's data would look like this:

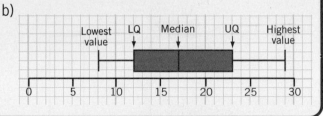

Example
The times taken (in minutes) to finish an assault course are listed in order.

8, 12, (12), 13, 15, (17) 22, 23, (23) 27, 29
   LQ   Median   UQ

From the data find...
a) (i) the lower quartile
   (ii) the interquartile range
b) Draw a box plot for this data.

a) (i) 12 (ii) UQ – LQ = 23 – 12 = 11
b)

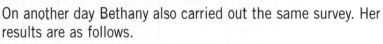

QUICK TEST

On another day Bethany also carried out the same survey. Her results are as follows.

① Draw a cumulative frequency graph of the grid below.

② Work out:
   a) the median
   b) interquartile range for Bethany's data.

Distance (d miles)	Frequency
$0 \leqslant d < 5$	15
$5 \leqslant d < 10$	60
$10 \leqslant d < 15$	67
$15 \leqslant d < 20$	30
$20 \leqslant d < 25$	22
$25 \leqslant d < 30$	6

Histograms

A *histogram* is similar to a bar chart except that the bars can be of different widths. The frequency is represented by the area of each bar, rather than its length or height.

Drawing histograms

When the bars have different widths the vertical axis is known as the **frequency density** where:

$$\text{frequency density} = \frac{\text{frequency}}{\text{class width}}$$

Then the areas of the rectangles are proportional to the frequencies that they represent.

Frequency = frequency density × class width

Example

The table shows the times, in seconds, it takes people to swim 100 metres. Draw a histogram of this information.

Time, (*t* seconds)	Frequency
$100 < t \leqslant 110$	2
$110 < t \leqslant 140$	24
$140 < t \leqslant 160$	42
$160 < t \leqslant 200$	50
$200 < t \leqslant 220$	24
$220 < t \leqslant 300$	20

To draw a histogram you need to calculate the frequency densities. Add an extra column to the table. Draw the histogram on graph paper. Make sure that there are no gaps between the columns.

Time, (*t* seconds)	Frequency	Frequency density
$100 < t \leqslant 110$	2	$2 \div 10 = 0.2$
$110 < t \leqslant 140$	24	$24 \div 30 = 0.8$
$140 < t \leqslant 160$	42	$42 \div 20 = 2.1$
$160 < t \leqslant 200$	50	$50 \div 40 = 1.25$
$200 < t \leqslant 220$	24	$24 \div 20 = 1.2$
$220 < t \leqslant 300$	20	$20 \div 80 = 0.25$

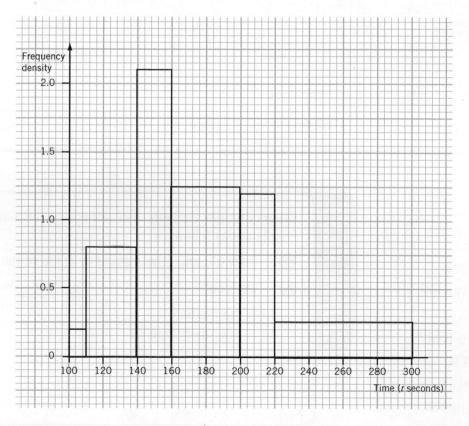

Interpreting histograms

Sometimes you may be given a histogram and asked to use the information given in it to complete the frequency table.
In order to do this it is best to find the area of each bar by using:

Frequency = frequency density × class width

Example

The histogram below gives information about the ages of some runners in a marathon. Use the information in the histogram to complete the table.

Age (A years)	Frequency
$0 \leqslant A < 20$	20
$20 \leqslant A < 30$	30
$30 \leqslant A < 40$	45
$40 \leqslant A < 60$	60
$60 \leqslant A < 100$	48

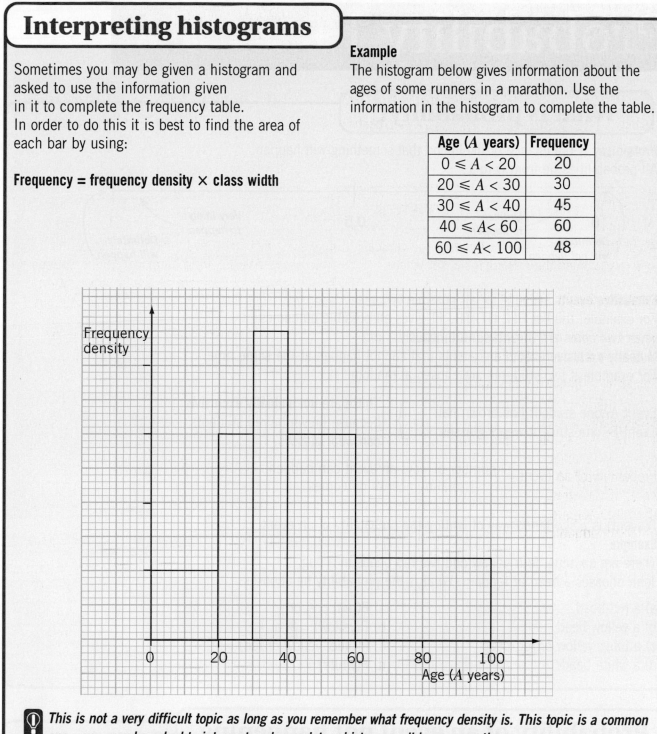

> This is not a very difficult topic as long as you remember what frequency density is. This topic is a common one – you may be asked to interpret and complete a histogram all in one question.

KEY TERMS

Make sure you understand these terms before moving on!
- histogram
- frequency density
- class width

QUICK TEST

1. Draw a histogram for the following information.

Number of hours (h)	Frequency
$0 \leqslant h < 20$	40
$20 \leqslant h < 30$	5
$30 \leqslant h < 60$	15
$60 \leqslant h < 70$	10
$70 \leqslant h < 100$	15

101

Probability 1

What is probability?

Probability is the chance or likelihood that something will happen.
All probabilities lie from 0 to 1.

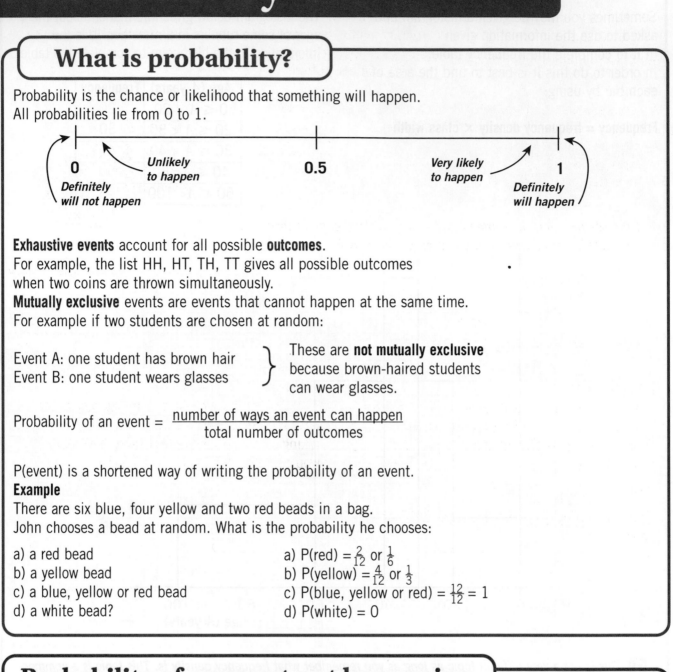

Exhaustive events account for all possible **outcomes**.
For example, the list HH, HT, TH, TT gives all possible outcomes
when two coins are thrown simultaneously.
Mutually exclusive events are events that cannot happen at the same time.
For example if two students are chosen at random:

Event A: one student has brown hair
Event B: one student wears glasses
} These are **not mutually exclusive** because brown-haired students can wear glasses.

$$\text{Probability of an event} = \frac{\text{number of ways an event can happen}}{\text{total number of outcomes}}$$

P(event) is a shortened way of writing the probability of an event.

Example
There are six blue, four yellow and two red beads in a bag.
John chooses a bead at random. What is the probability he chooses:

a) a red bead
b) a yellow bead
c) a blue, yellow or red bead
d) a white bead?

a) $P(\text{red}) = \frac{2}{12}$ or $\frac{1}{6}$
b) $P(\text{yellow}) = \frac{4}{12}$ or $\frac{1}{3}$
c) $P(\text{blue, yellow or red}) = \frac{12}{12} = 1$
d) $P(\text{white}) = 0$

Probability of an event not happening

If two outcomes of an event are **mutually exclusive**, then

P (outcome will happen) = 1 − P (outcome will not happen)

or

P (outcome will not happen) = 1 − P (outcome will happen)

Example
The probability that someone gets flu next winter is 0.42. What is the probability that they do not get flu next winter?
P(not get flu) = 1 − P(get flu)
= 1 − 0.42
= 0.58

Example
The probability that it will rain on any given day in August is $\frac{3}{11}$. What is the probability that it will not rain on a given day?

P(will not rain) = 1 − P(will rain)
= $1 - \frac{3}{11}$
= $\frac{8}{11}$

Relative frequencies

Relative frequencies are used to estimate probability.
If it is not possible to calculate a probability, an experiment can be used to find the relative frequency.

Relative frequency of an event = $\dfrac{\text{number of times event occurred}}{\text{total number of trials}}$

Example
When a fair die was thrown 80 times a six came up 12 times.
What is the relative frequency of getting a six?
number of trials = 80
number of sixes = 12
relative frequency = $\frac{12}{80}$ = 0.15

 Probabilities must be written as a fraction, decimal or percentage.
Probabilities can never be negative or greater than 1.

Expected number

Example
If a fair die is thrown 300 times, approximately how many fives are likely to be obtained?
There are six possible outcomes and all are equally likely.

P(5) = $\frac{1}{6}$ × 300 = 50 fives

Multiply 300 by $\frac{1}{6}$ since a 5 is expected $\frac{1}{6}$ of the time.

Example
The probability of passing a driving test at the first attempt is 0.65. If there are 200 people taking their test for the first time, how many would you expect to pass the test?

0.65 × 200 = 130 people

KEY TERMS

Make sure you understand these terms before moving on!
- exhaustive events
- outcomes
- mutually exclusive

QUICK TEST

1. Write down an event that will have a probability of zero.

2. A box contains three salt and vinegar, four cheese and two bacon flavoured packets of crisps. If a packet of crisps is chosen at random what is the probability that it is:
   a) salt and vinegar   b) cheese   c) onion flavoured?

3. The probability that it will not rain tomorrow is $\frac{2}{9}$. What is the probability that it will rain tomorrow?

4. The probability of achieving a grade C in Mathematics is 0.48. If 500 students sit the exam how many would you expect to achieve a grade C?

5. When a fair die was thrown 200 times, a five came up 47 times. What was the relative frequency of getting a five?

Probability 2

The multiplication law

- When two events are **independent** the outcome of the second event is not affected by the outcome of the first.
- If two or more events are **independent**, the probability of A and B and C . . . happening together is found by **multiplying** the separate probabilities.

P(A and B and C . . .) = P(A) × P(B) × P(C) . . .

Example

The probability that it will rain on any day in August is $\frac{3}{10}$. Find the probability that:

a) it will rain on both 1 August and 3 August

b) it will rain on 9 August but not 20 August.

a) P (rain and rain) = $\frac{3}{10} \times \frac{3}{10} = \frac{9}{100}$

b) P (rain and not rain) = $\frac{3}{10} \times \frac{7}{10} = \frac{21}{100}$

The addition law

If two or more events are **mutually exclusive** the probability of A or B or C . . . happening is found by **adding** the probabilities.

P (A or B or C. . .) = P(A) + P(B) + P(C) + . . .

Example

There are 11 counters in a bag. Five of the counters are red and three of them are white.

Lucy picks a counter at random. Find the probability that Lucy's counter is either red or white.

P(red) = $\frac{5}{11}$

P(white) = $\frac{3}{11}$

P(red or white) = P(red) + P(white)

$\frac{5}{11} + \frac{3}{11}$　Red and white are mutually exclusive.

= $\frac{8}{11}$

Sample space

When you are considering outcomes of two events it can be helpful to draw a table. This kind of table is sometimes known as a **sample space diagram**.

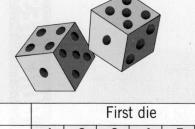

Example

Two dice are thrown together and their scores are added. Draw a diagram to show all the outcomes. Find the probability of:

a) a score of 7

b) a score that is a multiple of 4

a) P(score of 7) = $\frac{6}{36} = \frac{1}{6}$

b) P(multiple of 4) = $\frac{9}{36} = \frac{1}{4}$

There are 36 possible outcomes

		First die					
		1	2	3	4	5	6
Second die	1	2	3	4	5	6	7
	2	3	4	5	6	7	8
	3	4	5	6	7	8	9
	4	5	6	7	8	9	10
	5	6	7	8	9	10	11
	6	7	8	9	10	11	12

Tree diagrams

Tree diagrams are another way of showing the possible outcomes of two or more events. They may be written horizontally or vertically.

Example
In a class, the probability that a pupil will own a television is $\frac{5}{7}$ and the probability that the pupil will own a computer is $\frac{1}{4}$. These two events are independent.

Draw a tree diagram for this information.
- Draw the first branch, which shows the probabilities of having televisions.
- Put the probabilities on the branches.
- Draw the second branches, which show the probabilities of having computers.

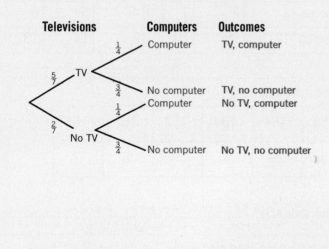

The multiplication and addition laws are useful when answering questions about tree diagrams.

a) Find the probability that a pupil will have their own TV and a computer.

P(TV and computer)
$\quad$ = P(TV) × P(computer)
$\quad$ = $\frac{5}{7} \times \frac{1}{4}$
$\quad$ = $\frac{5}{28}$

b) Find the probability that a pupil will have only one of the items.

P(TV and no computer) = P(TV) × P(no computer)
$\quad$ = $\frac{5}{7} \times \frac{3}{4}$
$\quad$ = $\frac{15}{28}$

OR

P(no TV and computer) = P(no TV) × P(computer)
$\quad$ = $\frac{2}{7} \times \frac{1}{4}$
$\quad$ = $\frac{2}{28}$

P(only one of the items) = $\frac{15}{28} + \frac{2}{28}$ = $\frac{17}{28}$

> **When answering questions that involve tree diagrams remember to:**
> - **make sure that on each pair of branches the probabilities add up to 1**
> - **multiply along the branches**
> - **add the probabilities when there is more than one alternative, i.e. P(A or B).**

KEY TERMS

Make sure you understand these terms before moving on!
- independent event
- mutually exclusive
- sample space diagram
- tree diagram

QUICK TEST

1. The probability that Meena does her homework is 0.8. The probability that Fiona does her homework is 0.45. Find the probability that both girls do their homework.

2. a) Draw a sample space diagram that shows the outcomes when two dice are thrown together and their scores are multiplied.
   b) What is the probability of a score of 6?
   c) What is the probability of a score of 37?

3. A bag contains three red and four blue counters. If a counter is taken out of the bag at random, its colour noted and then it is replaced, and a second counter is taken out, what is the probability of choosing one counter of each colour? (Use a tree diagram to help you.)

Practice questions

Use these questions to test your progress. Check your answers on page 111. You may wish to answer these questions on a separate piece of paper so that you can show full working out.

1. The probability that Josie gets full marks in a tables test is 0.82. What is the probability that she does not get full marks in the tables test?

   ....

2. A youth club has 75 members, of which 42 are boys. There are 15 members who are boys under 13 years old. There are 21 members who are girls over 13 years old.
   a) Complete the two-way table.
   b) How many of the girls are under 13 years old?

	Under 13 years old	13 years old and over	Totals
Boys			
Girls			
Total			

3. The probability of passing a driving test is 0.7. If 200 people take the test today, how many would you expect to pass?

   ....

4. Michelle is a swimmer. The probability of her winning a race is 84%. If she swims in 50 races this season, how many races would you expect her to win?

   ....

5. A die is thrown and the scores are noted. The results are shown in this table. Work out the mean die score.

Die score	1	2	3	4	5	6
Frequency	12	15	10	8	14	13

   ....

6. In a survey the heights of ten girls and their shoe sizes were measured.

Height in cm	150	157	159	161	158	164	154	152	162	168
Shoe size	3	5	$5\frac{1}{2}$	6	5	$6\frac{1}{2}$	4	$3\frac{1}{2}$	6	7

   a) Draw a scatter diagram to illustrate this data.
   b) What type of correlation is there between height and shoe size? ....
   c) Draw a line of best fit on your diagram. ....
   d) From your scatter diagram, estimate the height of a girl whose shoe size is $4\frac{1}{2}$. ....

   ....

7. The mass of some students in a class are measured. These are the results.
   a) Work out an estimate for the mean weight of the students.

   ....

   b) What is the modal class? ....

Mass (W kg)	Number of students
$40 \leqslant W < 45$	6
$45 \leqslant W < 50$	5
$50 \leqslant W < 55$	8
$55 \leqslant W < 60$	4
$60 \leqslant W < 65$	2

8. Ahmed and Matthew are going to take a swimming test. The probability that Ahmed will pass the swimming test is 0.85. The probability that Matthew will pass the swimming test is 0.6. The two events are independent.
   a) Complete the probability tree diagram.
   b) Work out the probability that both Ahmed and Matthew will pass the swimming test.

   ....

   c) Work out the probability that one of them will pass the swimming test and the other will not pass the swimming test.

   ....

9. The table shows the times, in minutes, for 83 people's journeys to work.
   a) Complete the cumulative frequency column in the table.
   b) Draw a cumulative frequency graph of the data.
   c) From your graph find the median.
   ....
   d) From your graph find the interquartile range.
   ....

Time (t minutes)	Frequency	Cumulative frequency
$0 \leqslant t < 10$	5	
$10 \leqslant t < 20$	20	
$20 \leqslant t < 30$	26	
$30 \leqslant t < 40$	18	
$40 \leqslant t < 50$	10	
$50 \leqslant t < 60$	4	

   e) How many people had a journey of more than 45 minutes to work? .... **C**
   ....

10. The table shows the working life of 60 batteries.
    Draw a histogram of this information.

Number of hours (h)	Frequency
$0 \leqslant h < 5$	9
$5 \leqslant h < 20$	15
$20 \leqslant h < 30$	18
$30 \leqslant h < 50$	10
$50 \leqslant h < 60$	8

11. A bag contains four red and three green beads. A bead is taken from the bag at random, and then replaced. A second bead is then taken. What is the probability that:
    a) both beads are red ....
    b) the beads are different colours? ....
    ....

12. There are 1200 pupils at a school. The table shows how they are distributed by year group.

Year	Number of pupils
7	180
8	265
9	245
10	210
11	300

    Emily is conducting a survey about pupil's favourite sports. She decides to use a stratified random sample of 200 pupils. How many students in each year group does she need to sample?
    ....

13. A bag contains three yellow and five blue beads. A bead is taken from the bag at random and not replaced. A second bead is then taken. What is the probability that:
    a) both beads are blue? ....
    b) the beads are different colours? ....

C *Indicates that a calculator may be used.*

How well did you do? X 0–3 Try again 4–6 Getting there 7–9 Good work 10–13 Excellent! ✓

Answers

Number
Quick test answers

Page 5 Types of numbers

1. 2, 3, 5, 7, 11, 13, 17, 19
2. HCF: 12; LCM: 120
3. a) ± 8 b) 6
4. a) $\frac{12}{9}$ b) $\frac{p}{x}$

Page 7 Positive and negative numbers

1. 3°C
2. a) 4 b) –16 c) –12 d) –12 e) 5 f) 6 g) 7 h) –10 i) 36

Page 9 Fractions

1. 1. a) $\frac{1}{3}$ b) $\frac{7}{20}$ c) $\frac{6}{13}$ d) $1\frac{1}{3}$ e) $\frac{5}{21}$ f) $\frac{4}{21}$ g) $\frac{49}{121}$ h) $\frac{50}{63}$ 2. £40 3. 247mm

Page 11 Decimals

1. a) 36.48 b) 17.679 c) 26.88 d) 12.3 e) 6 f) 52 g) 0.4 h) 0.0037 i) 4000
   j) 45000 k) 470000 l) 32500
2. a) 7.47 b) 12.04 c) 9.37 d) 10.04 e) 8.18

Page 13 Percentages 1

1. £210   2. 74.6%   3. 9.9 lb   4. £411.76   5. Super's; £33.33

Page 15 Percentages 2

1. £289   2. a) £1800 b) £6180   3. £100440   4. £3496.73

Page 16 Equivalents

1. i)a) 0.2857 b) 28.57% (2 d.p.) ii)a) 0.6 b) 60% iii)a) 0.8$\dot{8}$ b) 88.8$\dot{8}$%
2. 0.041, 5%, 26%, $\frac{1}{3}$, $\frac{2}{5}$, 0.42

Page 17 Using a calculator

1. a) 14.45 (2 d.p.)   b) 769.6 (1 d.p.)   c) 7.052 (3 d.p.)   d) $8\frac{1}{3}$ or 8.$\dot{3}$

Page 19 Approximating and checking calculations

1. a) 0.00379 b) 27500 c) 307000   2. 100   3. 10 rolls   4. £4.75

Page 21 Ratio

1. a) 4 : 5 b) 1 : 2 c) 5 : 2
2. 10, 15 and 35 sweets respectively
3. £2.76
4. 36 cm

Page 23 Indices

1. a) 12^{12} b) 9^{-6} c) 1 d) 18^8 e) 4^{10} f) 1
2. a) x^{13} b) $6x^{13}$ c) $4x^2$ d) $5x^{11}$ e) $2x^{12}$
3. a) 16 b) $\frac{1}{125}$ c) 12 d) $\frac{1}{6}$
4. a) $\frac{1}{16x^2}$ b) $\frac{1}{36x^4y^8}$

Page 25 Standard index form

1. a) 6.3 x 10^5 b) 2.73 x 10^3 c) 4.29 x 10^{-5} d) 6.3 x 10^{-7}
2. a) 6 x 10^{12} b) 1.22 x 10^9 c) 4 x 10^3 d) 3 x 10^{18}
3. a) 4.35 x 10^{10} b) 4.59 x 10^{16}
4. 9.76 x 10^{10}

Page 26 Diverse and inverse proprtion

1. $y = 1$ (equation: $y = \frac{100}{x^2}$)
2. $p = 21$ (equation: $p = 3\sqrt{t}$)

3. $r = 1.587$ (equation: $s = \frac{40}{r^3}$)

Page 27 Recurring decimals and surds

1. a) $\frac{15}{99} = \frac{5}{33}$ b) $\frac{7}{9}$ c) $\frac{281}{990}$
2. a) $5\sqrt{3}$ b) $10\sqrt{5}$ c) $11 - 6\sqrt{2}$ d) $4\sqrt{2} - \sqrt{6} + 18$
3. $\frac{\sqrt{3}}{3}$

Page 29 Upper and lower bounds of measurement

1. upper bound = 0.65 (2 d.p.) lower bound = 0.64 $\therefore$ $0.64 \leqslant x < 0.65$
2. upper bound = 56.375 lower bound = 51.675 $\therefore$ $51.675 \leqslant x < 56.375$

Pages 30–31 Answers to practice questions

1. £25000
2. a) 365 b) 0.706
3. $\dfrac{9+9}{0.2 \times 50} = \dfrac{18}{10} = 1.8$
4. The 100 ml tube of toothpaste.
5. 1.5 cm
6. £376.47
7. £6502.50
8. £715.02
9. 20%
10. a) 2.67×10^6 b) 4.27×10^3 c) 3.296×10^{-2} d) 2.7×10^{-2}
11. a) 4.2×10^{-5} g b) 2.52×10^1 g
12. a) 1.2×10^{22} b) 2 x 10^{11}
13. a) $y = 3x$
    b) $x = 6.\dot{6}$
14. $y = \frac{20}{x^2}$ a) $y = 1\frac{1}{4}$ b) $x = \sqrt{2} = (1.414...)$
15. a) $\frac{4}{9}$ b) $\frac{21}{99} = \frac{7}{33}$ c) $\frac{234}{999} = \frac{26}{111}$ d) $\frac{25}{90} = \frac{5}{18}$
16. a) $2\sqrt{3}$ b) $5\sqrt{3}$ c) $10\sqrt{2}$ d) $3\sqrt{2} - 2\sqrt{6}$ e) 15
17. Upper bound = 2.301375 m^2
    Lower bound = 2.271075 m^2
18. Upper bound = 13.28 m/s (2 d.p.)
    Lower bound = 13.04 m/s (2 d.p.)
19. Upper bound = 6.7349 cm (4 d.p.)
    Lower bound = 6.7112 cm (4 d.p.)
20. a) 4 b) 4 c) $\frac{1}{36}$ d) 7 e) $\frac{1}{5}$ f) $\frac{1}{16}$ g) $\frac{49}{25}$

Algebra
Quick test answers

Page 33 Algebra 1

1. a) $10a$ b) $8a + b$ c) $9x + 4y$ d) $4x^2y - 5xy^2$
2. a) –16.84 b) 118.52 c) 8.17$\dot{3}$ d) 475.24

Page 35 Algebra 2

1. a) $3x + 6$ b) $2x + 2y$ c) $-6x - 12$ d) $x^2 + 5x + 6$ e) $y^2 - 7y + 12$
   f) $a^2 + 4a + 4$
2. a) $3(x + 3)$ b) $5(y - 3)$ c) $6x(2x - 1)$ d) $(x - 6)(x + 1)$ e) $(x - 1)(x - 2)$
   f) $(x - 4)(x + 4)$
3. $u = \pm\sqrt{v^2 - 2as}$
4. $R = \frac{V}{I}$

Page 37 Equations 1

1. $x = 6$ 2. $x = 4.5$ 3. $x = 2$ 4. $x = 4$ 5. $x = -1$ 6. $x = -1.4$
7. $x = 1, x = -5$ 8. $x = 2, x = 3$ 9. $k = 1\frac{3}{4}$

Page 39 Equations 2

1. a) $x = -4.5, y = 4$ b) $a = 2, b = 1$
2. $x = 3, y = -1$
3. 3.3

Page 41 Further algebra and equations

1. a) $x = \frac{1}{3}, x = 2$ b) $x = -\frac{1}{2}, x = -2$ c) $x = -\frac{1}{4}, x = 2$
2. $r = \frac{-(y + ps)}{(p - 1)}$ or $\frac{(y + ps)}{(1 - p)}$
3. a) $\frac{5x + 4}{(x + 2)(x - 1)}$ b) $\frac{(s + 2)(s - 1)}{6(s - 3)}$ c) $\frac{18(a + b)(a + 1)}{(a + 2)}$

Page 42 Inequalities

1. $x < 6$
2. $x \geqslant 4$
3. $1 \leqslant x \leqslant 3$
4. $\frac{-1}{5} \leqslant x < 2$

Page 43 Number Patterns and Sequences

1. a) 13, 15 b) 25, 36 c) 4, 2
2. a) $2n + 3$ b) $3n - 1$ c) $4n + 2$ d) $10 - 2n$

Page 45 Straight line graphs

1. a) $x = 1$ b) $x = 1.5$
2. a) Gradient 2; Intercept (0, 4) b) Gradient 3; Intercept (0, –2)
   c) Gradient 3; Intercept (0, 2)

Page 47 Curved graphs

1. a)

x	–3	–2	–1	0	1	2	3
y	–24	–5	2	3	4	11	30

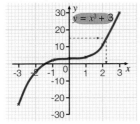

b) The coordinates that need to be plotted are:
(3, 30), (2, 11), (1, 4), (0, 3), (–1, 2), (–2, –5), (–3, –24)
c) When $y = 15$, $x = 2.3$ (to 1 d.p.)

2. Graph A: $y = 3 - x^2$ Graph B: $y = \frac{2}{x}$ Graph C: $y = 5 - x$ Graph D: $y = x^3$

Page 49 Harder work on graphs

1.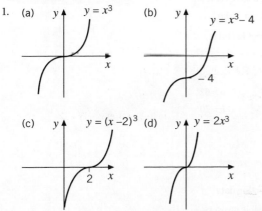

2. $x = -1, y = 1$ $x = 4, y = 16$

Page 51 Interpreting graphs

1. Container A graph 3; Container B graph 1; Container C graph 2
2. a) $x = -2.8, 1.8$ b) $x = -1.4, 1.4$ c) $x = 2.7, -0.7$

Pages 52–53 Answers to practice questions

1. a) $x = 3$ b) $x = 4$ c) $x = 5$ d) $x = 2$ e) $x = 1$
2. $2n^2 + 1$
3. a) $12x^4$ b) $12x^5 y^3$
   c) $4y^3$ d) $9y^4$
4. $a = 3, b = -2$
5. $P = 54.3$ (3 s.f.) b) $y = \frac{P^2 + 3x^2}{5x}$
6. $x = 1.8$
7. $1 \leqslant n \leqslant 3$
8. A is $(y = 3 - 4x)$ B is $(y = 2x + 1)$
   C is $(xy = 6)$ D is $(y = x^2 - 4)$
9. a) $\frac{5x + 8}{(x + 4)(x - 2)}$ b) $\frac{4x + 30}{(x - 3)(x + 4)}$ c) $\frac{1}{2}$
10. $(x - 2)(2x - 9) = 0$ $\therefore x = 2$ $x = \frac{9}{2}$
11. a) $x = 1.721, x = -0.387$
    b) $x = 0.8385, x = -0.2385$
12. a) $(x - 2)^2 - 3 = 0$ b) $(x - 4)^2 - 6 = 0$
    $x = 3.732$ $x = 6.449$
    $x = 0.268$ $x = 1.551$
13. a) $(2x + 4)(x - 1) = 50$
    $2x^2 + 2x - 4 = 50$
    $2x^2 + 2x - 54 = 0$
    $x^2 + x - 27 = 0$
    b) $x = 4.72$
    Length = 13.44 cm
14. $x = 0$ $y = 4$
    $x = -4$ $y = 0$
    The line $y = x + 4$ intersects the circle
    $x^2 + y^2 = 16$ at (0, 4) and (–4, 0).
15. $p = \frac{4x - 2r}{6 + x}$
16. a) Move graph 2 units to left.
    b) Move graph 3 units down the y-axis.
    c) Reflect the graph in the x axis.
    d) Multiply all x values by $\frac{1}{2}$.
17. a = 6   b = 1.414

Shape, space and measures
Quick test answers

Page 55 Constructions

a) 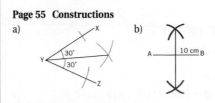 b)

Page 57 Angles

1. a) $a = 150°$ b) $b = 70°, c = 110°, d = 70°$
   c) $a = 50°, b = 50°,\ c = 130°, d = 50°$
2. a) 72° b) 108°

Page 59 Bearings and scale drawings

1. a) 072° b) 305° c) 145°
2. a) 252° b) 125° c) 325°
3. 7 km

Page 61 Transformations 1

1.
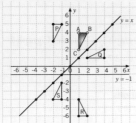

2. Move 2 to the left and 3 upwards

Page 63 Transformations 2

1.

2.
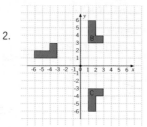

Page 65 Similarity and congruency

1. a) 7.8 cm b) 9.1 cm

2. 15.9 cm

3. Yes, because SAS, i.e. 2 sides and included angle are equal.

4. Area = 90 cm^2

Page 66 Loci and coordinates in 3D

1.

Page 67 Angle properties of circles

1. $a = 84°$; $b = 20°$; $c = 94°$; $d = 86°$

Page 69 Pythogoras' theorem

1. a) 17.2 cm b) 20.0 cm

2. 17 cm

3. 94.3 km

Page 71 Trigonometry in right-angled triangles

1.

2. a) 7.5 cm b) 10.1 cm c) 18 cm 3. a) 25.6° b) 62.3° c) 36.9°

Page 73 Application of trigonometry

1. 35.8 m (3 s.f.)

2. a) 20 cm b) 68.0 cm c) 17.1°

3. a) HF = 25 cm b) Angle CHF = 11.3°

Page 75 Further trigonometry

1. a) 8.08 cm b) 28.4º c) 28.0º d) 68.83 cm 2. 41.8º, 138.2º

Page 77 Measures and measurement

1. 3.5 kg 2. 6.6 lb 3. 10½ pints 4. 9.15 ⩽ 9.2 < 9.25

5. 57.5 ⩽ 58 < 58.5 6. 2.25 m.p.h.

7. 8.57 hours (or 8 hours 34 minutes) 8. 2.2 g/cm^3

Page 79 Area of 2D shapes

1. a) 68.0 cm^2 (3 s.f.) b) 63.6 cm^2 (3 s.f.) c) 63.6 cm^2 (3 s.f.)

   d) 208 cm^2 (3 s.f.)

2. 21.5 cm^2 (3 s.f.)

Page 81 Volume of 3D shapes

1. a) 1750 cm^3 (3 s.f.) b) 60 100 cm^3 (3 s.f.)

2. 20.3 cm (3 s.f.)

3. a) Perimeter b) Volume c) Volume d) Area

Page 83 Further length, area and volume

1. Arc length = 13.96 cm. Sector area = 139.6 cm^2

2. 123 π cm^3

Page 85 Vectors

1. a) Since $\vec{AC} = \binom{6}{8}$ and $\vec{PQ} = \binom{3}{4}$ then $2\vec{PQ} = \vec{AC}$ so they are parallel.

   b) Ratio 2:1

2. a) $\vec{PR} = \mathbf{p} + \mathbf{q}$ b) $\vec{MQ} = \frac{1}{2}(\mathbf{p} - \mathbf{q})$

Pages 86–87 Answers to practice questions

1.
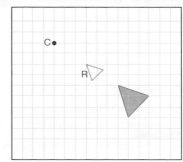

2. a) 122.5 m^2
   b) 63.6 cm^2

3. 52.5 mph

4. 5.2 m

5. 1.94 m^3

6. 9.2 m

7. a) 68°
   b) 3.65 cm
   c) 11.74 cm

8. $l\sqrt{r^2 + t^2}$; πr^2; $2tl$

9. Arc length = 4.80 cm
   Sector area = 12.0 cm

10. Volume = 697.43 cm^3

11. Radius = 3.99 cm (2 d.p.)

12. Surface area = 1920 cm^2

13. Volume = 113.1 cm^3

14. a) $-\mathbf{r} + \mathbf{t}$ b) $-\mathbf{r} + 2\mathbf{t}$ c) $-3\mathbf{r} + 2\mathbf{t}$

15. −300 degrees, −60 degrees, 60 degrees, 300 degrees

16. a) 12.32 m (2 d.p.)
    b) $x = 147.5$ degrees (1 d.p.)
    c) $x = 45.2$ degrees (1 d.p.)
    d) $x = 7.11$ cm (2 d.p.)

17. height = 81.4 m (1 d.p.)

18. (a) $a = 55°$ $b = 35°$
    (b) $a = 75°$ $b = 58°$
    (c) $a = 85°$ $b = 62°$
    (d) $a = 55°$ $b = 70°$

Handling data
Quick test answers

Page 89 Collecting data

1. Many possible answers

2. Yr 7 – 24 Yr 8 – 30 Yr 9 – 46

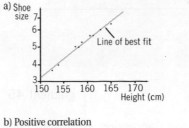

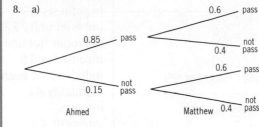

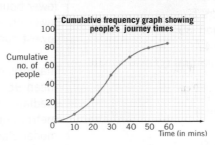

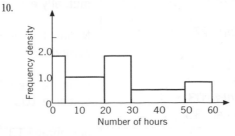

Page 91 Representing data

1. The angles for the pie chart are: Brown 120º, Auburn 60º, Blonde 90º, Black 90º

2. a) The frequencies for the heights are: $140 \leqslant h < 145 = 6$, $145 \leqslant h < 150 = 10$, $150 \leqslant h < 155 = 11$, $155 \leqslant h < 160 = 5$, $160 < h \leqslant 165 = 2$

   b) 34 people were in the survey

   c) The frequency polygon should be plotted at the midpoints of the bars.

Page 93 Scatter diagrams and correlation

1. a) Positive b) Zero c) Negative d) Negative

Page 95 Averages 1

1. mean = 5; median = 4; mode = 4; range = 7

2. a) mean = 1.32 mins b) median = 1 c) mode = 0 d) range = 4

Page 97 Averages 2

1. a) 151.56 b) $150 \leqslant h < 155$

Page 99 Cumulative frequency graphs

1. A cumulative frequency graph with the following points should be plotted: (5,15) (10,75) (15,142) (20,172) (25,194) (30,200).

2. a) median approx. 12 miles   b) interquartile range = 9 miles (approx.)

Page 101 Histograms

1.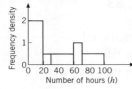

Page 103 Probability 1

1. Answers could be: I will get a 7 when I throw a die; or I will get a 4 when I throw a coin. 2. a) $\frac{1}{3}$ b) $\frac{4}{9}$ c) 0 3. $\frac{7}{9}$ 4. 240 5. $\frac{47}{200}$

Page 105 Probability 2

1. 0.36

2. a)

		1	2	3	4	5	6
	1	1	2	3	4	5	6
	2	2	4	6	8	10	12
Die 2	3	3	6	9	12	15	18
	4	4	8	12	16	20	24
	5	5	10	15	20	25	30
	6	6	12	18	24	30	36

Die 1

   b) $\frac{4}{36} = \frac{1}{9}$ c) 0

3. $\frac{24}{49}$

Pages 106–107 Answers to practice questions

1. 0.18

2. a)

	Under 13 yrs	13 yrs+	Totals
Boys	15	27	42
Girls	12	21	33
Total	27	48	75

   b) 12

3. 140 people

4. 42 races

5. 3.5

6. a)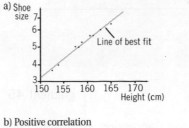

   b) Positive correlation

   c) See scatter diagram

   d) 155.5 cm

7. a) 50.7 kg b) $50 \leqslant W < 55$

8. a)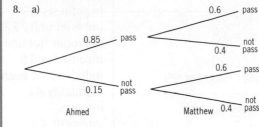

   b)   0.51

   c)   0.43

9. a)

Time (t min)	Frequency	Cumulative frequency
$0 \leqslant t < 10$	5	5
$10 \leqslant t < 20$	20	25
$20 \leqslant t < 30$	26	51
$30 \leqslant t < 40$	18	69
$40 \leqslant t < 50$	10	79
$50 \leqslant t < 60$	4	83

   b)

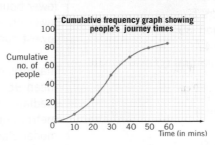

Cumulative frequency graph showing people's journey times

   c) Approx 26 min

   d) 18 min

   e) 8 people

10.

11. a) $\frac{16}{49}$ b) $\frac{24}{49}$

12. Yr 7   30

    Yr 8   44

    Yr 9   41

    Yr 10 35

    Yr 11 50

13. a) $\frac{20}{56} = \frac{5}{14}$

    b) $\frac{30}{56} = \frac{15}{28}$

Index

MATHS SUCCESS

Index